Travesties

by

Tom Stoppard

Grove Press, Inc., New York

First Evergreen Edition 1975
Fifth Printing 1977
ISBN: 0-394-17884-X
Grove Press ISBN: 0-8021-0098-8
Library of Congress Catalog Card Number: 75-13552

Manufactured in the United States of America

Distributed by Random House, Inc., New York

GROVE PRESS, INC., 196 West Houston Street, New York, N.Y. 10014

FOR OLIVER, BARNABY,
WILLIAM AND EDMUND

Characters

HENRY CARR, appears as a very old man and also as his youthful self. He dresses in a most elegant way and is especially interested in the cut of his trousers; he has the figure for it.

TRISTAN TZARA, is the Dadaist of that name. He was a short, dark-haired, very boyish-looking young man, and charming (his word). He wears a monocle.

JAMES JOYCE, is James Joyce in 1917/18, aged 36. He wears a jacket and trousers from two different suits.

LENIN, is Lenin in 1917: aged 47.

BENNETT, is Carr's manservant. Quite a weighty presence.

GWENDOLEN, is Carr's younger sister; young and attractive but also a personality to be reckoned with.

CECILY, is also young and attractive and even more to be reckoned with. Also appears as her old self.

NADYA, is Nadezhda Krupskaya, Lenin's wife: aged 48.

The first performance of *Travesties* took place at the Aldwych Theatre, London, on 10th June 1974 in a production by the Royal Shakespeare Company. The cast was as follows:

HENRY CARR	John Wood
TRISTAN TZARA	John Hurt
JAMES JOYCE	Tom Bell
LENIN	Frank Windsor
BENNETT	John Bott
GWENDOLEN	Maria Aitken
CECILY	Beth Morris
NADYA	Barbara Leigh-Hunt

The play was directed by Peter Wood, and designed by Carl Toms with lighting by Robert Ornbo.

The reader of a play whose principal characters include Lenin, James Joyce and Tristan Tzara may not realise that the figure of Henry Carr is likewise taken from history. But this is so.

In March 1918 (I take the following information from Richard Ellmann's *James Joyce*), Claud Sykes, an actor temporarily living in Zurich, suggested to Joyce that they form a theatrical company to put on plays in English. Joyce agreed, and became the business manager of The English Players, the first production to be that of *The Importance of Being Earnest*. Actors were sought. Professionals were to receive a token fee of 30 francs (24 shillings at the current rate of exchange) and amateurs to make do with 10 francs for tram fare to rehearsals. Joyce became very active and visited the Consul General, A. Percy Bennett, in order to procure official approval for the Players. He succeeded in this, despite the fact that Bennett "was annoyed with Joyce for not having reported to the Consulate officially to offer his services in wartime, and was perhaps aware of Joyce's work for the neutralist *International Review* and of his open indifference to the war's outcome. He may even have heard of Joyce's version of *Mr. Dooley*, written about this time . . ."—I quote from Ellmann's superb biography, whose companionship was not the least pleasure in the writing of *Travesties*.

Meanwhile, Sykes was piecing together a cast . . . "An important find was Tristan Rawson, a handsome man who had sung baritone roles for four years in the Cologne Opera House but had never acted in a play. After much coaxing Rawson agreed to take on the role of John Worthing. Sykes recruited Cecil Palmer as the butler, and found a woman named Ethel Turner to play Miss Prism . . . As yet, however, there was no one to take the leading role of Algernon Moncrieff. In an unlucky moment Joyce nominated a tall, goodlooking young man named Henry Carr, whom he had seen in the consulate. Carr, invalided from the service, had a small job there. Sykes learned that he had acted in some amateur plays in Canada, and decided to risk him."

Carr's performance turned out to be a small triumph. He had even, in his enthusiasm, bought some trousers, a hat and a pair of gloves to wear as Algernon. But immediately after the performance the actor and the business manager quarrelled. Joyce handed each member of the cast 10 or 30 francs, as pre-arranged, but succeeded in piquing Carr, who later complained to Sykes that Joyce had handed over the money like a tip.

The upshot was disproportionate and drawn out. Joyce and Carr ended up going to law, in two separate actions, Carr claiming reimbursement for the cost of the trousers, etc., or alternatively a share of the profits, and Joyce counter-claiming for the price of five tickets sold by Carr, and also suing for slander. These matters were not settled until February 1919. Joyce won on the money and lost on the slander, but he reserved his full retribution for *Ulysses*, where "he allotted punishments as scrupulously and inexorably as Dante . . . Originally Joyce intended to make Consul General Bennett and Henry Carr the two drunken, blasphemous and obscene soldiers who knock Stephen Dedalus down in the 'Circe' episode; but he eventually decided that Bennett should be the sergeant-major, with authority over Private Carr, who, however, refers to him with utter disrespect."

From these meagre facts about Henry Carr—and being able to discover no others—I conjured up an elderly gentleman still living in Zurich, married to a girl he met in the Library during the Lenin years, and recollecting, perhaps not with entire accuracy, his encounters with Joyce and the Dadaist Tzara.

Soon after the play opened in London I was excited and somewhat alarmed to receive a letter beginning, "I was totally fascinated by the reviews of your play—the chief reason being that Henry Carr was my husband until he died in 1962." The letter was from Mrs. Noël Carr, his second wife.

From her I learned that Henry Wilfred Carr was born in Sunderland in 1894 and brought up in County Durham. He was one of four sons, including his twin Walter, now also dead. At 17 Henry went to Canada where he worked for a time in a bank. In 1915 he volunteered for military service and went to France with the Canadian Black Watch. He was badly wounded the following year and—after lying five days in no-man's-land—was taken prisoner. Because of his wounds Henry was sent by the Germans to stay at a monastery where the monks tended him to a partial recovery, and then as an "exchange prisoner" he was one of a group who were sent to Switzerland.

Thus Henry Carr arrived in Zurich where he was to cross the path of James Joyce and find himself a leading actor in both onstage and offstage dramas, leading to immortality of a kind as a minor character in *Ulysses*.

It was in Zurich, too, that he met his first wife, Nora Tulloch. They married in England after the war and later he took her back to Canada where he found a job in a department store in Montreal. He rose within the organisation to become company secretary.

In 1928, while in Montreal, he met Noël Bach and after his divorce they were married there in 1933. The following year they returned to England. Henry ultimately joined a foundry company and when the next war came he and his wife were living in Sheffield. They were bombed out, and moved to a Warwickshire village, where Henry commanded the Home Guard, and they stayed in Warwickshire in the post-war years.

In 1962, while he was on a visit to London, Henry had a heart attack, and he died in St. Mary Abbots Hospital, Kensington. He had no children.

I am indebted to Mrs. Noël Carr for these biographical details, and, particularly, for her benevolence towards me and towards what must seem to her a peculiarly well-named play.

T.S.

Acknowledgements

Nearly everything spoken by Lenin and Nadezhda Krupskaya herein comes from his Collected Writings and from her *Memories of Lenin*. I have also profited variously—and gratefully—from the following books: *Lenin* by Michael C. Morgan; *Lenin* by Robert Payne; *Lenin and the Bolsheviks* by Adam B. Ulam; *To The Finland Station* by Edmund Wilson; *Days With Lenin* by Maxim Gorki; *The First World War, an Illustrated History* by A. J. P. Taylor; *James Joyce* by Richard Ellmann; *Joyce* by John Gross; *Dada, Art and Anti-Art* by Hans Richter; and *The Dada Painters and Poets*, edited by Robert Motherwell. I am also indebted to Mr. James Klugmann for material relating to Lenin in Switzerland. The responsibility for the use to which this and all other material is put is my own.

The play is set in Zurich, in two locations: the drawing room of Henry Carr's apartment ("THE ROOM"), and a section of the Zurich Public Library ("THE LIBRARY"). Most of the action takes place within Carr's memory, which goes back to the period of the First World War, and this period is reflected appropriately in the design and the costumes, etc. It is to be supposed that Old Carr has lived in the same apartment since that time.

The ROOM must have the main door Centre Upstage: most of the entrances would be weakened seriously if they occurred from the side. Double doors would be best. However, there is also at least one side door. There is a centre table with a good chair on each side, and a side table, apart from other furniture.

The LIBRARY suggests a larger scale—tall bookcases, etc. In Act Two Cecily (the librarian) requires a counter or desk, which need not necessarily be in view at the beginning of the play. Some of the entrances, e.g. Nadya's, should be through a door rather than from the wings.

The LIBRARY in the Prologue and the Second Act does not necessarily have to be presented from the same angle.

We begin in the LIBRARY

There are places for JOYCE, LENIN and TZARA.

GWEN sits with JOYCE. They are occupied with books, papers, pencils . . .

LENIN is also writing quietly, among books and papers. TZARA is writing as the play begins. On his table are a hat and a large pair of scissors. TZARA finishes writing, then takes up the scissors and cuts the paper, word by word, into his hat. When all the words are in the hat he shakes the hat and empties it on the table. He rapidly separates the bits of paper into random lines, turning a few over, etc., and then

17

reads the result in a loud voice.

TZARA: Eel ate enormous appletzara
key dairy chef's hat he'lllearn oomparah!
Ill raced alas whispers kill later nut east,
noon avuncular ill day Clara!

CECILY (*entering*): Sssssssh!

(*Her admonition is to the Library in general. She enters from one wing, not through the door, and crosses the stage, leaving by the opposite wing, moving quite quickly, like someone who is busy. No one takes any notice.*)

JOYCE (*dictating to* GWEN): Deshill holles eamus . . .

GWEN (*writing*): Deshill holles eamus . . .

JOYCE: Thrice.

GWEN: Uh-hum.

JOYCE: Send us bright one, light one, Horhorn, quickening and wombfruit.

GWEN: Send us bright one, light one, Horhorn, quickening and wombfruit.

JOYCE: Thrice.

GWEN: Uh-hum.

JOYCE: Hoopsa, boyaboy, hoopsa!

GWEN: Hoopsa, boyaboy, hoopsa!

JOYCE: Hoopsa, boyaboy, hoopsa!

GWEN: Likewise thrice?

JOYCE: Uh-hum.

(*By this time* TZARA *has replaced the bits of paper into the hat. He takes out a handful, and reads the words one at a time, placing them into the hat as he reads each one.*)

TZARA: Clara avuncular!
Whispers ill oomparah!
Eel nut dairy day
Appletzara . . .
. . . Hat!

CECILY (*re-entering*): Ssssssh!

(CECILY *has come in with a few books which she places by* LENIN.)

(TZARA *leaves the Library through the door.*)

(*It is now necessary that the audience should observe the*

following: GWEN *has received from* JOYCE *a folder.* CECILY
receives an identical folder from LENIN. *These folders,
assumed to contain manuscripts, are eye-catching objects in
some striking colour. Each girl has cause to place her folder
down on a table or chair, and each girl then picks up the
wrong folder. In the original production,* GWEN *dropped a
glove, etc., etc., but it is not important how this transference
is achieved, only that it is* seen *to occur.*)

(GWEN *is now ready to leave the Library, and does so, taking
Lenin's folder with her.*)

(CECILY *also leaves, not through the door but into the wings.*)

(NADYA *enters as* GWEN *leaves; They bump into each other,
and each apologises,* GWEN *in English,* NADYA *in Russian.*)

(NADYA *enters in an agitated state. She looks round for her
husband and goes straight to him. Their conversation is in
Russian.*)

NADYA: Vylodya!

LENIN: Shto takoya? (*What is it?*)

NADYA: Bronski prishol. On s'kazal shto v'Peterburge
revolutsia! (*Bronski came to the house. He says there's a
revolution in St. Petersburg.*)

LENIN: Revolutsia!

(*At this point* JOYCE *stands up and begins to walk up and
down searching his pockets for tiny scraps of paper on which
he has previously written down things he may wish to use.
While the Lenins continue their conversation,* JOYCE *fishes out,
one by one, these scraps of paper and reads out what he finds
on them.*)

JOYCE (*regarding his first find*): "Morose delectation . . .
Aquinas tunbelly . . . Frate porcospino . . ."

(*He decides he doesn't need this one. He screws it up and
throws it away, and finds a second . . .*)

"Und alle Schiffe brucken . . ."

(*He decides to keep this one, so re-pockets it. He takes out
another.*)

"Entweder transubstantiality, oder consubstantiality, but
in no way substantiality . . ."

(*He decides to keep this one as well. Meanwhile, the* LENINS *have been continuing in the following manner*):

LENIN: Otkuda on znayet? (*How does he know?*)

NADYA: Napisano v'Gazetakh. On govorit shto Tsar sobiraet'sia otretchsya ot prestola! (*It's all in the papers. He says the Tsar is going to abdicate!*)

LENIN: Shtoty! (*No!*)

NADYA: Da! (*Yes!*)

LENIN: Eto v'gazetakh? (*Is that in the newspaper?*)

NADYA: Da—da. Idiom damoi. On zhdyot. (*Yes—yes. Come on home. He's waiting.*)

LENIN: On tam? (*Is he there?*)

NADYA: Da! (*Yes!*)

LENIN: Gazetakh u nievo? (*He brought the paper?*)

NADYA: Da! (*Yes!*)

LENIN: Ty sama vidyela? (*You saw it yourself?*)

NADYA: Da, da, da! (*Yes, yes, yes!*)

(JOYCE'S *voice, however, has dominated this passage. He now encounters a further scrap of paper which is lying on the floor:* LENIN *has inadvertently dropped it.* JOYCE *picks this paper up.* NADYA *is leaving the Library, through the door,* LENIN *saying in Russian* . . .)

LENIN: Idyi nazad y skazhee y'moo shto ya prichazhoo. Tolka pasbyrayu svayi b'magi. (*Go home ahead of me. I will collect my papers and follow.*)

(LENIN *is gathering his papers.* JOYCE *is examining the dropped paper.*)

JOYCE: "G.E.C. (U.S.A.) 250 million marks, 28,000 workers . . . profit 254,000,000 marks . . ."

(LENIN *recognises these words. He pauses, and approaches* JOYCE.)

LENIN: Pardon! . . . Entschuldigung! . . . Scusi! . . . Excuse me!

JOYCE (*handing him the paper*): Je vous en prie! Bitte! Prego! It's perfectly all right!

(LENIN *leaves.* JOYCE *is alone now.*)

(*declaims*) A librarianness of Zurisssh
only emerged from her niche
when a lack of response
to *Nicht Reden! Silence!*

20

obliged her to utter the plea——

CECILY (*entering as before*): —sssssssh!

(JOYCE *accedes to her request, puts on his hat, picks up his stick, and while she regards him with disapproval he leaves at a strolling pace, singing . . .*)

JOYCE: If you ever go across the sea to Ireland . . .

It may be at the closing of the day . . .

you can sit and watch the moon rise over Claddagh

and watch the sun go down on Galway Bay . . .

(*The stage now belongs to* OLD CARR. *The* LIBRARY *must now be replaced by the* ROOM. *Needless to say, the change should occur with as little disruption as possible, and the use of music as a bridge is probably desirable.*)

(*NOTE: In the original production, the Room contained a piano which was at different times used by Old Carr, and in this instance Old Carr played (very badly) the tune of Galway Bay while the set was changed; the piano being right downstage in a permanent position. It is possible that* CARR *has been immobile on stage from the beginning, an old man remembering . . .*)

CARR: He was Irish, of course. Though not actually from Limerick—he was a Dublin man, Joyce, everybody knows that, couldn't have written the book without. There was a young man from Dublin, tum-ti-ti-tum-ti-ti troublin' . . . I used to have quite a knack for it, but there's little encouragement for that sort of thing in the Consular Service. Not a great patron of poetry, the Service, didn't push it, never made a feature of it. I mean you'd never say that a facility for rhyme and metre was the sine qua non of advancement in the Consular Service . . . Didn't *dis*courage it, I'm not saying that, on the contrary, a most enlightened and cultivated body of men, fully sympathetic to all the arts (look no further than the occasion that brought us together, me and Joyce, brought him to this room, full support, a theatrical event of the first water, great success, personal triumph in the demanding role of Ernest, not Ernest, the other one, in at the top, have we got the cucumber sandwiches for Lady Bracknell, notwithstanding the unfortunate consequences. Irish lout. Not one to bear a grudge, however, not after all these years, and him dead in the cemetery up the hill, no hard feelings either side, unpleasant as it is to be dragged through the courts for a few francs (though it wasn't the money, or the trousers for that matter), *but*, be that as it may, all in all, truth be told, the encouragement of poetry writing, was not the primary concern of the British Consulate in Zurich in 1917, and now I've lost my knack for it. Too late to go back for it. Alas and alack for it. But I digress. No apologies required, constant digression being the saving grace of senile reminiscence.

My memoirs, is it, then? Life and times, friend of the famous. Memories of James Joyce. James Joyce As I Knew Him. The James Joyce I Knew. Through the Courts With James Joyce . . . What was he like, James Joyce, I am often asked. It is true that I knew him well at the height of his powers, his genius in full flood in the making of *Ulysses*, before publication and fame turned him into a public monument for pilgrim cameras more often than not in a velvet smoking jacket of an unknown colour, photography being in those days a black and white affair, but probably real blue if not empirical purple and sniffing a bunch of sultry violets that positively defy development, don't go on, do it on my head, caviar for the general public, now then— *Memories of James Joyce* . . . It's coming.

To those of us who knew him, Joyce's genius was never in doubt. To be in his presence was to be aware of an amazing intellect bent on shaping itself into the permanent form of its own monument—the book the world now knows as *Ulysses*! Though at that time we were still calling it (I hope memory serves) by its original title, Elasticated Bloomers.

A prudish, prudent man, Joyce, in no way profligate or vulgar, and yet convivial, without being spend-thrift, and yet still without primness towards hard currency in all its transmutable and transferable forms and denominations, of which, however, he demanded only a sufficiency from

the world at large, exhibiting a monkish unconcern for
worldly and bodily comforts, without at the same time
shutting himself off from the richness of human society,
whose temptations, on the other hand, he met with an ascetic
disregard tempered only by sudden and catastrophic
aberrations—in short, a complex personality, an enigma, a
contradictory spokesman for the truth, an obsessive litigant
and yet an essentially private man who wished his total
indifference to public notice to be universally recognised—
in short a liar and a hypocrite, a tight-fisted, sponging,
fornicating drunk not worth the paper, that's that bit done.

Further recollections of a Consular Official in Whitest
Switzerland. The Ups and Downs of Consular life in
Zurich During the Great War: A Sketch.
'Twas in the bustling metropolis of swiftly gliding trams
and greystone banking houses, of cosmopolitan restaurants
on the great stone banks of the swiftly-gliding snot-green
(mucus mutandis) Limmat River, of jewelled escapements
and refugees of all kinds, e.g. Lenin, there's a point . . .
Lenin As I Knew Him. The Lenin I Knew. Halfway to
the Finland Station with V. I. Lenin: A Sketch, I well
remember the first time I met Lenin, or as he was known
on his library ticket, Vladimir Ilyich Ulyanov. To be in
his presence was to be aware of a complex personality,
enigmatic, magnetic, but not, I think, astigmatic, his
piercing brown (if memory serves) eyes giving no hint of it.
An essentially simple man, and yet an intellectual
theoretician, bent, as I was already aware, on the seemingly
impossible task of reshaping the civilised world into a
federation of standing committees of workers' deputies.
As I shook the hand of this dynamic, gnomic and yet not,
I think, anaemic stranger, who with his fine head of blond
hair falling over his forehead had the clean-shaven look of
a Scandinavian seafaring—hello, hello, got the wrong chap,
has he?—take no notice, all come out in the wash, that's
the art of it. Fact of the matter, *who* (without benefit of
historical perspective and the photograph album, Red
Square packed to the corner stickers with comraderaderie,

23

and now for our main speaker, balding bearded in the
three-piece suit, good God if it isn't Ulyanov!, knew him
well, always sat between the window and Economics
A–K etceterarera) well, take away all *that*, and who was he
to Radek or Radek to him, or Martov or Martinov,
Plekhanov, or he to Ulyanov for that matter?—in Zurich
in 1917? Café conspirators, so what? Snowballs in hell.
Snowballs at all, Lenin he only had one chance in a
million, remember the time they had the meeting?—Social
Democrats for Civil War in Europe. Total attendance:
four. Ulyanov, Mrs. Ulyanov, Zinoviev and a police spy.
And now they want to know what was he like? What was
he like, Lenin, I am often asked.

(*He makes an effort*).

To those of us who knew him Lenin's greatness was
never in doubt.

(*He gives up again.*)

So why didn't you put a pound on him, you'd be a
millionaire, like that chap who bet sixpence against the
Titanic. No. Truth of the matter, who'd have thought big
oaks from a corner room at number 14 Spiegelgasse?—
now here's a thing: two revolutions formed *in the same
street*. Face to face in Spiegelgasse! *Street of Revolution!
A sketch.* Meet by the sadly-sliding chagrinned Limmat
River, strike west and immediately we find ourselves soaking
wet, strike east and immediately we find ourselves in the
Old Town, having left behind the banking bouncing
metropolis of trampolines and chronometry of all kinds for
here time has stopped in the riddled maze of alleyways and
by the way you'd never believe a Swiss redlight district,
pornographic fretwork shops, vice dens, get a grip on
yourself, sorry, sorry, second right, third left—
Spiegelgasse!—narrow, cobbled, high old houses in a solid
rank, number 14 the house of the narrow cobbler himself,
Kammerer his name, Lenin his tenant—
and across the way at Number One, the Meierei Bar,
crucible of anti-art, cradle of Dada!!! Who? What?
Whatsisay Dada?? You remember Dada!—historical halfway

house between Futurism and Surrealism, twixt Marinetti and André Breton, 'tween the before-the-war-to-end-all-wars years and the between-the-wars years—*Dada!*—down with reason, logic, causality, coherence, tradition, proportion, sense and consequence, my art belongs to Dada 'cos Dada 'e treats me so—well then, *Memories of Dada by a Consular Friend of the Famous in Old Zurich: A Sketch.*

What did it do in the Great War, Dada, I am often asked. How did it begin? where did it? when? what was it, who named it and why Dada? These are just some of the questions that continue to baffle Dadaists the world over. To those of us who lived through it Dada was, topographically speaking, the high point of Western European culture—I well remember as though it were yesteryear (oh where are they now?) how Hugo Ball—or was it Hans Arp? yes!—no—Picabia, was it?—no, Tzara—yes!—wrote his name in the snow with a walking stick and said: There! I think I'll call it The Alps. Oh the yes-no's of yesteryear. Whose only age done gone. Over the hills and far away the sixpounders pounding in howitzerland, no louder than the soft thud of snow falling off the roof—*oh heaven!* to be picked out—plucked out—blessed by the blood of a negligible wound and released into the folds of snow-covered hills—Oh, Switzerland!—unfurled like a white flag, pacific civilian Switzerland—the miraculous neutrality of it, the non-combatant impartiality of it, the non-aggression pacts of it, the international red cross of it—entente to the left, detente to the right, into the valley of the invalided blundered and wandered myself when young——

Carr of the Consulate!—first name Henry, that much is beyond dispute, I'm mentioned in the books.

For the rest I'd be willing to enter into discussion but not if you don't mind correspondence, into matters of detail and chronology—I stand open to correction on all points, except for my height which can't be far off, and the success of my performance, which I remember clearly, in the demanding role of Ernest (not Ernest, the other one)——

that, and the sense of sheer relief at arriving in a state of rest, namely Switzerland, the still centre of the wheel of war. That's really the thing——

(CARR *is now a young man in his drawing room in 1917. Ideally the actor should simply take off e.g. a hat and dressing gown—no wig or beard, no make-up—Carr's age has been in his voice.*)

—the first thing to grasp about Switzerland is that there is no war here. Even when there is war *everywhere else*, there is no war in Switzerland.

BENNETT: Yes, sir.

(BENNETT *has entered with a tray of tea things, set for two, with sandwiches.*)

CARR: It is this complete absence of bellicosity, coupled with an ostentatious punctuality of public clocks, that gives the place its reassuring air of permanence. Switzerland, one instinctively feels, will not go away. Nor will it turn into somewhere else. You have no doubt heard allusions to the beneficial quality of the Swiss air, Bennett. The quality referred to is permanence.

BENNETT: Yes, sir.

CARR: Desperate men who have heard the clocks strike thirteen in Alsace, in Trieste, in Serbia and Montenegro, who have felt the ground shift beneath them in Estonia, Austro-Hungary and the Ottoman Empire, arrive in Switzerland and after a few deep breaths find that the ringing and buzzing in their ears has regulated itself into a soothing tick-tock, and that the ground beneath their feet, while invariably sloping, is as steady as an alp. Tonight I incline to the theatre; get me out the straight cut trouser with the blue satin stripe and the silk cutaway. I'll wear the opal studs.

BENNETT: Yes, sir. I have put the newspapers and telegrams on the sideboard, sir.

CARR: Is there anything of interest?

BENNETT: The *Neue Zuricher Zeitung* and the *Zuricher Post* announce, respectively, an important Allied and German victory, each side gaining ground after inflicting heavy casualties on the other with little loss to itself.

CARR: Ah—yes . . . the war! Poor devils! How I wish I could get back to the trenches!—to my comrades in arms—the wonderful spirit out there in the mud and wire—the brave days and fearful nights. Bliss it was to see the dawn! To be alive was very heaven! Never in the whole history of human conflict was there anything to match the carnage—God's blood!, the shot and shell!—graveyard stench!—Christ Jesu!—deserted by simpletons, they damn us to hell—ora pro nobis—quick! no, *get me out!*—I think to match the carnation, oxblood shot-silk cravat, starched, creased just so, asserted by a simple pin, the damask lapels—or a brown, no, biscuit—no—get me out the straight cut trouser with the blue satin stripe and the silk cutaway. I'll wear the opal studs.

BENNETT: Yes, sir. I have put the newspapers and telegrams on the sideboard, sir.

CARR: Is there anything of interest?

BENNETT: The war continues to dominate the newspapers, sir.

CARR: Ah yes . . . the war, always the war . . .

(*A note on the above: the scene (and most of the play) is under the erratic control of Old Carr's memory, which is not notably reliable, and also of his various prejudices and delusions. One result is that the story (like a toy train perhaps) occasionally jumps the rails and has to be restarted at the point where it goes wild.*

This scene has several of these "time slips", indicated by the repetitions of the exchange between BENNETT *and* CARR *about the "newspapers and telegrams". Later in the play there are similar cycles as Carr's memory drops a scene and then picks it up again with a repeated line (e.g.* CARR *and* CECILY *in the Library). It may be desirable to mark these moments more heavily by using an extraneous sound or a light effect, or both. The sound of a cuckoo-clock, artificially amplified, would be appropriate since it alludes to time and to Switzerland; in which case a naturalistic cuckoo-clock could be seen to strike during the here-and-now scene of Old Carr's first monologue. At any rate the effect of these time-slips is not meant to be bewildering, and it should be made clear what is happening.*)

I was in Savile Row when I heard the news, talking to the
head cutter at Drewitt and Madge in a hounds-tooth
check slightly flared behind the knee, quite unusual. Old
Drewitt, or Madge, came in and told me. Never trusted
the Hun, I remarked. Boche, he replied, and I, at that time
unfamiliar with the appellation, turned on my heel and
walked into Trimmett and Punch where I ordered a
complete suit of Harris knicker-bockers with hacking vents.
By the time they were ready, I was in France. Great days!
Dawn breaking over no-man's-land. Dewdrops glistening
on the poppies in the early morning sun—All quiet on the
We tern Front . . .Tickety boo, tickety boo, tickety boo . . .

BENNETT: A gentleman called, sir. He did not wait.

CARR: What did he want?

BENNETT: He did not vouchsafe his business, sir. He left his card.
(*Offers it on a salver.*)

CARR: "Tristan Tzara. Dada Dada Dada." Did he have a stutter?

BENNETT: He spoke French with a Rumanian accent, and wore
a monocle.

CARR: He is obviously trying to pass himself off as a spy. It is a
form of vanity widely indulged in in Zurich during a European
war, I believe, and adds greatly to the inconveniences
caused by the crowds of *real* spies who conspire to fill the
Odeon and the Terrasse, and make it almost impossible to
get a table at either.

BENNETT: I have noticed him with a group of friends at the
Terrasse, sir. Whether they were conspirators I could not,
of course, tell.

CARR: To masquerade as a conspirator, or at any rate to speak
French with a Rumanian accent and wear a monocle, is at
least as wicked as to be one; in fact, rather more wicked,
since it gives a dishonest impression of perfidy, and,
moreover, makes the over-crowding in the cafés gratuitous,
being the result neither of genuine intrigue nor bona fide
treachery—was it not, after all, La Rochefoucauld in his
Maximes who had it that in Zurich in Spring in wartime
a gentleman is hard put to find a vacant seat for the
spurious spies peeping at police spies spying on spies

eyeing counter-spies *what a bloody country even the cheese has got holes in it!!*

(*Off the rails again.* CARR *has, on the above words, done violence to the inside of a cheese sandwich.*)

BENNETT: Yes, sir. I have put the newspapers and telegrams on the sideboard, sir.

CARR: Is there anything of interest?

BENNETT: There is a revolution in Russia, sir.

CARR: Really? What sort of revolution?

BENNETT: A social revolution, sir.

CARR: A *social* revolution? Unaccompanied women smoking at the Opera, that sort of thing? . . .

BENNETT: Not precisely that, sir. It is more in the nature of a revolution of classes contraposed by the fissiparous disequilibrium of Russian society.

CARR: What do you mean, classes?

BENNETT: Masters and servants. As it were. Sir.

CARR: Oh. Masters and servants. *Classes.*

BENNETT (*expressionless as always*): There have been scenes of violence.

CARR: I see. Well, I'm not in the least bit surprised, Bennett. I don't wish to appear wise after the event, but anyone with half an acquaintance with Russian society could see that the day was not far off before the exploited class, disillusioned by the neglect of its interests, alarmed by the falling value of the rouble, and above all goaded beyond endurance by the insolent rapacity of its servants, should turn upon those butlers, footmen, cooks, valets . . . (parenthetically, Bennett, I see from your book that on Thursday night when Mr. Tzara was dining with me, eight bottles of champagne are entered as having been consumed. I have had previous occasion to speak to you of the virtues of moderation, Bennett: this time I will only say, remember Russia).

BENNETT: Yes, sir. I have put the newspapers and telegrams on the sideboard, sir.

CARR: Is there anything of interest?

BENNETT: The Tsar has now abdicated, sir. There is a Provisional Government headed by Prince Lvov, with

Guchkov as Minister of War, Milyukov Foreign Minister and the Socialist Kerensky as Minister of Justice. The inclusion of Kerensky is calculated to recommend the Government to a broad base of the common people, but effective authority has already been challenged by a committee of workers' deputies, or "Soviet", which has for the moment united all shades of socialist opinion. However there is no immediate prospect of the Socialists seizing power, for the revolution is regarded by them as the fulfilment of Karl Marx's prophecy of a *bourgeois capitalist era* in Russia's progress towards socialism. According to Marxist dogma, there is no way for a country to leap from autocracy to socialism: while the *ultimate* triumph of socialism is inevitable, being the necessary end of the process of dialectical materialism, it must, by the same token, be preceded by a bourgeois-capitalist stage of development. When the time is ripe, and not before, there will be a further revolution, led by the organised industrial workers, or "Proletariat", who will assume a temporary dictatorship to ensure the safe transition of the State into a true Communist Utopia. Thus, it is the duty of Russian Marxists to welcome the present bourgeois revolution, even though it might take several generations to get through, if the examples of Western Europe and the United States are anything to go by. As things stand, therefore, if one can be certain of anything it is that Russia is set fair to become a parliamentary democracy on the British model.

CARR: Newspapers or coded telegram?

BENNETT: A consensus of the most recent London dailies and political and humorous weeklies, and general rumour put about Zurich by the crowds of spies, counter-spies, radicals, artists and riff-raff of all kinds. Mr. Tzara called, sir. He did not wait.

CARR: I'm not sure that I approve of your taking up this modish novelty of "free association", Bennett. I realise that it is all the rage in Zurich—even in the most respectable salons to try to follow a conversation nowadays is like reading every other line of a sonnet—but if the servant classes are

30

going to ape the fashions of society, the end can only be ruin and decay.

BENNETT: I'm sorry, sir. It is only that Mr. Tzara being an artist——

CARR: I will not have you passing moral judgements on my friends. If Mr. Tzara is an artist that is his misfortune.

BENNETT: Yes, sir. I have put the newspapers and telegrams on the sideboard, sir.

CARR: Is there anything of interest?

BENNETT: In St. Petersburg, the Provisional Government has now declared its intention to carry on the war, and has gained the sympathy of the British and the French. However, the committee of workers' deputies, or Soviet, consider the war to be nothing more than an imperialist adventure carried on at the expense of workers of both sides. To co-operate in this adventure is to be stigmatised in a novel phrase which seems to translate as a "lickspittle capitalist manservant", unnecessarily offensive in my view.

CARR (*languidly*): I'm not sure that I'm much interested in your views, Bennett.

BENNETT (*apologetically*): They're *not* particularly interesting, sir. However, the Soviet has ordered soldiers and sailors to ignore the orders of the Provisional Government; this has won it the corresponding sympathy of the Germans. However, unity of the Left is not now complete. There is a more extreme position put forward by the Bolshevik party. The Bolshevik line is that some unspecified but unique property of the Russian situation, unforeseen by Marx, has caused the bourgeois-capitalist era of Russian history to be compressed into the last few days, and that the time for the proletarian revolution is now ripe. Furthermore, the Bolsheviks say the soldiers should shoot all the officers and turn the war into a European civil war. However, the Bolsheviks are a small minority in the Soviet, and their leader, Vladimir Ulyanov, also known as Lenin, has been in exile since the abortive 1905 revolution, and is in fact living in Zurich.

CARR: Naturally.

BENNETT: Yes, sir—if I may quote La Rochefoucauld, "Quel pays sanguinaire, même le fromage est plein des trous." Lenin is desperately trying to return to Russia but naturally the Allies will not allow him free passage. Since Lenin is almost alone in proclaiming the Bolshevik orthodoxy, which is indeed his creation, his views at present count for nothing in St. Petersburg, where ostensible Bolsheviks like Kamenev and Stalin are taking a moderate line. A betting man would lay odds of about a million to one against Lenin's view prevailing. However, it is suggested that you take all steps to ascertain his plans.

CARR: A consensus of the humorous and intellectual weeklies?

BENNETT: Telegram from the Minister.

(*He starts to leave.*)

CARR: A million to one.

BENNETT: I'd put a pound on him, sir.

CARR: You know him?

BENNETT: I do, sir. And if any doubt remained, the London papers carry the assurance that the man to watch is Kerensky.

(*Exit* BENNETT.)

CARR (*aside*): Bennett seems to be showing alarming signs of irony. I have always found that irony among the lower orders is the first sign of an awakening social consciousness. It remains to be seen whether it will grow into an armed seizure of the means of production, distribution and exchange, or spend itself in liberal journalism.

BENNETT (*entering*): Mr. Tzara.

(TZARA *enters.* BENNETT *retires.*)

CARR: How are you, my dear Tristan. What brings you here?

(*This Tzara (there is to be another) is a Rumanian nonsense. His entrance might be set to appropriate music.*)

TZARA (*ebulliently*): Plaizure, plaizure! What else? Eating ez usual, I see 'Enri?!—'allo—'allo, vhat is all the teapots etcetera? Somebody comink? It is Gwendolen I hopp!—I luff 'er, 'Enri—I have come by tram expressly to propose a marriage—ah—ha!——

BENNETT (*entering*): Miss Gwendolen and Mr. Joyce.

32

(GWENDOLEN *and* JAMES JOYCE *enter.* BENNETT *remains by the door.* GWENDOLEN *and* TZARA *are momentarily transfixed by each other. This is hardly noticed as* JOYCE *has made it his own entrance.*)

JOYCE: Top o' the morning!—James Joyce!
I hope you'll allow me to voice
my regrets in advance
for coming on the off-chance—
b'jasus I hadn't much choice!

(*This* JOYCE *is obviously an Irish nonsense. The whole scene is going to take a limerick form, so for clarity's sake the lay-out of the text is modified.*)

CARR: I . . . sorry . . . would you say that again?

JOYCE: Begob—I'd better explain
I'm told that you are a——

TZARA: Miss Carr!

GWEN: Mr. Tzara!

JOYCE: (*seeing* TZARA *for the first time*) B'jasus'. Joyce is the
name.

GWEN: I'm sorry!—how terribly rude!
Henry—Mr. Joyce!

CARR: How d'you do?

JOYCE: Delighted!

TZARA: Good day!

JOYCE: I just wanted to say
how sorry I am to intrude.

CARR: Tell me . . . are you some kind of a poet?

JOYCE: You know my work?

CARR: No—it's
something about your deliv'ry—
can't quite——

JOYCE: Irish.

CARR: From Lim'rick?

JOYCE: No—Dublin, don't tell me you know it!

GWEN: He's a poor writer——

JOYCE: Aha!
A fine writer who writes caviar
for the general, hence poor——

33

TZARA: Wants to touch you for sure.

JOYCE: I'm addressing my friend, Mr . . .

CARR: (*gulp*)   Carr.

GWEN: Mr. Tzara writes poetry and sculpts,
with quite unexpected results.
I'm told he recites
and on Saturday nights
does all kinds of things for adults.

JOYCE: I really don't think Mr. Carr
is interested much in da-dah——

TZARA: We say it like Dah-da.

JOYCE: (*to* CARR) The fact is I'm rather
hard up.

CARR: Yes I'm told that you are.
If it's money you want, I'm afraid . . .

GWEN: Oh, Henry!—he's mounting a play,
and Mr. Joyce thought
your official support . . .

CARR: Ah . . . !

JOYCE: And a couple of pounds till I'm paid.

CARR: I don't see why not. For my part,
H.M.G. is considered pro-Art.

TZARA: Consider me anti.

GWEN: Consider your auntie?

JOYCE: A pound would do for a start.

CARR: The Boche put on culture a-plenty
for Swiss, what's the word?

JOYCE: Cognoscenti.

CARR: It's worth fifty tanks

JOYCE: Or twenty-five francs

CARR: Now . . . British culture . . .

JOYCE: I'll take twenty.

TZARA: (*scornful*) Culture and reason!

JOYCE: Fifteen.

TZARA: They give us the mincing machine!

GWEN: That's awf'ly profound.

JOYCE: Could you lend me a pound?

TZARA: All literature is obscene!

34

The classics—tradition—vomit on it!

GWEN: (Oh!)

TZARA: Beethoven! Mozart! I spit on it!

GWEN: (Oh!)

TZARA: Everything's chance!

GWEN: Consider your aunts.

TZARA: Causality—logic—I sssssh——

GWEN: —awf'ly profound

JOYCE: (*to* BENNETT) Could you lend me a pound?

GWEN: I thought he was going to say "Shit on it".

(*Her hand flies, too late, to her mouth.* CARR *has been thinking hard.*)

CARR: By jove, I've got it! Iolanthe!

TZARA: Obscene!

CARR: Is it?

TZARA: Avanti!

        Gut'n tag! Adios!

GWEN: Au revoir!

TZARA: Vamanos!

BENNETT: Give my regards to your auntie.

(BENNETT *closes the door behind* TZARA *and* GWEN.)

(*The whole thing has been manic from beginning to end, and now it's finished, except that* JOYCE *is a leftover.*)

JOYCE: A Rumanian rhymer I met
    used a system he based on roulette.
    His reliance on chance
    was a def'nite advance
    and yet . . . and yet . . . and yet . . .

(*The light steps down between verses.*)

    An impromptu poet of Hibernia
    rhymed himself into a hernia
    He became quite adept
    at the practice except
    for occasional anti-climaxes.

    When I want to leave things in the air
    I say, "Excuse me, I've got to repair
    to my book about Bloom—"

and just leave the room.

(*He has gone. Pause. Low light on motionless* CARR *in his chair*.)

CARR: Well, let us resume. *Zurich By One Who Was There.*
(*Normal light.*)

BENNETT (*entering*): Mr. Tzara.

(TZARA *enters.* BENNETT *retires.*)

CARR: How are you, my dear Tristan? What brings you here?

TZARA: Oh, pleasure, pleasure! What else should bring anyone anywhere?

(TZARA, *no less than* CARR, *is straight out of* The Importance of Being Earnest.)

CARR: I don't know that I approve of these Benthamite ideas, Tristan. I realise they are all the rage in Zurich—even in the most respectable salon, to remark that one was brought there by a sense of duty, leads to terrible scenes but if society is going to ape the fashions of philosophy, the end can only be ruin and decay.

TZARA: Eating and drinking, as usual, I see, Henry? I have often observed that Stoical principles are more easily borne by those of Epicurean habits.

CARR (*stiffly*): I believe it is done to drink a glass of hock and seltzer before luncheon, and it is well done to drink it well before luncheon. I took to drinking hock and seltzer for my nerves at a time when nerves were fashionable in good society. This season it is trenchfoot, but I drink it regardless because I feel much better after it.

TZARA: You might have felt much better anyway.

CARR: No, no—post hock, propter hock.

TZARA: But, my dear Henry, causality, is no longer fashionable owing to the war.

CARR: How illogical, since the war itself had causes. I forget what they were, but it was all in the papers at the time. Something about brave little Belgium, wasn't it?

TZARA: Was it? I thought it was Serbia . . .

CARR: Brave little Serbia . . . ? No, I don't think so. The newspapers would never have risked calling the British public to arms without a proper regard for succinct alliteration.

TZARA: Oh, what nonsense you talk!

CARR: It may be nonsense, but at least it is clever nonsense.

TZARA: I am sick of cleverness. The clever people try to impose a design on the world and when it goes calamitously wrong they call it fate. In point of fact, everything is Chance, including design.

CARR: That sounds awfully clever. What does it mean? Not that it has to mean anything, of course.

TZARA: It means, my dear Henry, that the causes we know everything about depend on causes we know very little about, which depend on causes we know absolutely nothing about. And it is the duty of the artist to jeer and howl and belch at the delusion that infinite generations of real effects can be inferred from the gross expression of apparent cause.

CARR: It is the duty of the artist to beautify existence.

TZARA (*articulately*): Dada dada dada dada dada dada dada dada dada dada dada dada dada dada dada dada dada dada dada dada dada dada dada dada dada dada dada dada dada dada dada dada dada dada dada.

CARR (*slight pause*): Oh, what nonsense you talk!

TZARA: It may be nonsense, but at least it's not clever nonsense. Cleverness has been exploded, along with so much else, by the war.

CARR: You forget that I was there, in the mud and blood of a foreign field, unmatched by anything in the whole history of human carnage. Ruined several pairs of trousers. Nobody who has not been in the trenches can have the faintest conception of the horror of it. I had hardly set foot in France before I sank in up to the knees in a pair of twill jodphurs with pigskin straps handstitched by Ramidge and Hawkes. And so it went on—the sixteen ounce serge, the heavy worsteds, the silk flannel mixture—until I was invalided out with a bullet through the calf of an irreplaceable lambswool dyed khaki in the yarn to my own specification. I tell you, there is nothing in Switzerland to compare with it.

TZARA: Oh, come now, Henry, your trousers always look——

CARR: I mean with trench warfare.

37

TZARA: Well, I daresay, Henry, but you could have spent the time in Switzerland as an artist.

CARR (*coldly*): My dear Tristan, to be an artist *at all* is like living in Switzerland during a world war. To be an artist *in Zurich, in 1917*, implies a degree of self-absorption that would have glazed over the eyes of Narcissus. When I sent round to Hamish and Rudge for their military pattern book, I was responding to feelings of *patriotism, duty,* to my love of freedom, my hatred of tyranny and my sense of oneness with the underdog—I mean in general, I never particularly cared for the Belgians as such. And besides I couldn't be an artist *anywhere*—I can do none of the things by which is meant Art.

TZARA: Doing the things by which is meant Art is no longer considered the proper concern of the artist. In fact it is frowned upon. Nowadays, an artist is someone who makes art mean the things he does. A man may be an artist by exhibiting his hindquarters. He may be a poet by drawing words out of a hat. In fact some of my best poems have been drawn out of my hat which I afterwards exhibited to general acclaim at the Dada Gallery in Bahnhofstrasse.

CARR: But that is simply to change the meaning of the word Art.

TZARA: I see I have made myself clear.

CARR: Then you are not actually *an artist* at all?

TZARA: On the contrary. I have just told you I am.

CARR: But that does not make you an artist. An artist is someone who is gifted in some way that enables him to do something more or less well which can only be done badly or not at all by someone who is not thus gifted. If there is any point in using language at all it is that a word is taken to stand for a particular fact or idea and not for other facts or ideas. I might claim to be able to fly . . . Lo, I say, I am flying. But you are not propelling yourself about while suspended in the air, someone may point out. Ah no, I reply, that is no longer considered the proper concern of people who can fly. In fact, it is frowned upon. Nowadays, a flyer never leaves the ground and wouldn't know how. I see, says my somewhat baffled interlocutor, so when you

say you can *fly* you are using the word in a purely private
sense. I see I have made myself clear, I say. Then, says
this chap in some relief, you cannot actually *fly* after all?
On the contrary, I say, I have just told you I can. Don't
you see my dear Tristan you are simply asking me to accept
that the word Art means whatever you wish it to mean;
but I do not accept it.

TZARA: Why not? You do exactly the same thing with words
like *patriotism, duty, love, freedom,* king and country,
brave little Belgium, saucy little Serbia——

CARR (*coldly*): You are insulting my comrades-in-arms, many
of whom died on the field of honour——

TZARA: —and honour—all the traditional sophistries for waging
wars of expansion and self-interest, presented to the people
in the guise of rational argument set to patriotic hymns . . .
Music is corrupted, language conscripted. Words are taken
to stand for opposite facts, opposite ideas. That is why
anti-art is the art of our time.

(*The argument becomes progressively more heated.*)

CARR: The nerve of it. Wars are fought to make the world safe
for artists. It is never quite put in those terms but it is a
useful way of grasping what civilised ideals are all about.
The easiest way of knowing whether good has triumphed
over evil is to examine the freedom of the artist. The
ingratitude of artists, indeed their hostility, not to mention
the loss of nerve and failure of talent which accounts for
"modern art", merely demonstrate the freedom of the artist
to be ungrateful, hostile, self-centred and talentless, for
which freedom I went to war, and a more selfless ideal for
a man of my taste it would be difficult to imagine.

TZARA: Wars are fought for oil wells and coaling stations; for
control of the Dardanelles or the Suez Canal; for colonial
pickings to buy cheap in and conquered markets to sell
dear in. War is capitalism with the gloves off and many who
go to war know it but they go to war because they don't
want to be a hero. It takes courage to sit down and be
counted. But how much better to live bravely in Switzerland
than to die cravenly in France, quite apart from what it

does to one's trousers.

CARR: My God, you little Rumanian wog—you bloody dago
—you jumped-up phrase-making smart-alecy arty-
intellectual Balkan turd!!! Think you know it all!—while
we poor dupes think we're fighting for ideals, you've got a
profound understanding of what is *really* going on, underneath!—you've got a phrase for it! You pedant! Do you
think your phrases are the true sum of each man's living
of each day?—*capitalism with the gloves off?*—do you think
that's the true experience of a wire-cutting party caught in
a crossfire in no-man's-land?—Why not infantile sexuality
in khaki trews? Or the collective unconscious in a tin hat?
(*viciously*) It's all the rage in Zurich!—You slug! I'll tell
you what's *really* going on: I went to war because it was
my *duty*, because my country needed me, and that's
patriotism. I went to war because I believed that those
boring little Belgians and incompetent Frogs had the right
to be defended from German militarism, and that's *love of
freedom*. *That's* how things are underneath, and I won't
be told by some yellow-bellied Bolshevik that I ended up
in the trenches because there's a profit in ball-bearings!

TZARA (*storming*): *Quite right!* You ended up in the trenches,
because on the 28th of June 1900 the heir to the throne
of Austro-Hungary married beneath him and found that
the wife he loved was never allowed to sit next to him on
royal occasions, except! when he was acting in his military
capacity as Inspector General of the Austro-Hungarian
army—in which capacity he therefore decided to inspect
the army in Bosnia, so that *at least on their wedding
anniversary*, the 28th of June 1914, they might ride side
by side in an open carriage through the streets of
Sarajevo! (*sentimentally*) Aaaaah! (*then slaps his hands sharply
together like a gun-shot*) Or, to put it another way——

CARR (*quietly*): We're here because we're here . . . because we're
here because we're here . . . we're here because we're here
because we're here because we're here . . .

(CARR *has dropped into the familiar chant, quite quiet.*
TZARA *joins in, just using the sound "da-da" to the same tune.*

40

The light starts to go. The chant grows. When CARR *starts to speak,* TZARA *continues the chanting quietly for a few more moments under* CARR's *words.*)

Great days! The dawn breaking over no-man's-land—Dewdrops glistening on the poppies in the early morning sun! The trenches stirring to life! . . . "Good morning, corporal! All quiet on the Western Front?" . . . "Tickety-boo, sir!"—"Carry on!"—Wonderful spirit in the trenches—never in the whole history of human conflict was there anything to match the courage, the comradeship, the warmth, the cold, the mud, the stench—fear—folly—Christ Jesu!, but for this blessed leg!—I never thought to be picked out, plucked out, blessed by the blood of a blighty wound—oh *heaven!*—released into folds of snow-white feather beds, pacific civilian heaven!, the mystical swissticality of it, the entente cordiality of it!, the Jesus Christ I'm out of it!—into the valley of the invalided—Carr of the Consulate!

(*Lights to normal.*)

And what brings *you* here, my dear Tristan?

TZARA: Oh, pleasure, pleasure . . . What else should bring anyone anywhere? Eating as usual, I see, Henry?

CARR: I believe it is customary in good society to take a cucumber sandwich at five o'clock. Where have you been since last Thursday?

TZARA: In the Public Library.

CARR: What on earth were you doing there?

TZARA: That's just what I kept asking myself.

CARR: And what was the reply?

TZARA: "Ssssh!" Cecily does not approve of garrulity in the Reference Section.

CARR: Who is Cecily? And is she as pretty and well-bred as she sounds? Cecily is a name well thought of at fashionable christenings.

TZARA: Cecily is a librarianness. I say, do you know someone called Joyce?

CARR: *Joyce* is a name which could only expose a child to comment around the font.

TZARA: No, no, Mr. Joyce, Irish writer, mainly of limericks, christened James Augustine, though registered, due to a clerical error, as James Augusta, a little known fact.

CARR: Certainly I did not know it. But then I have never taken an interest in Irish affairs. In fashionable society it would be considered a sign of incipient vulgarity with radical undertones.

TZARA: The war caught Joyce and his wife in Trieste in Austro-Hungary. They got into Switzerland and settled in Zurich. He lives in Universitatsstrasse, and is often seen round about, in the library, in the cafés, wearing, for example, a black pinstripe jacket with grey herringbone trousers, or brown Donegal jacket with black pinstripe trousers, or grey herringbone jacket with brown Donegal trousers, all being the mismatched halves of sundry sundered Sunday suits: sorts language into hands of contract bridge; looks down on Dada, though his own poems reek of old hat, being second-hand fin-de-siècle slop. His limericks are said to be more interesting, though hardly likely to start a revolution—I say, do you know someone called Ulyanov?

CARR: I'm finding this conversation extremely hard to follow. It's like hearing every other line of the Catechism. And you still have not told me what you were doing in the public library. I had no idea that poets nowadays were interested in literature. Or is it that your interest is in Cecily?

TZARA: Good heavens, no. Cecily is rather pretty, and well-bred, as you surmised, but her views on poetry are very old-fashioned and her knowledge of the poets, as indeed of everything else, is eccentric, being based on alphabetical precedence. She is working her way along the shelves. She has read Allingham, Arnold, Belloc, Blake, both Brownings, Byron, and so on up to, I believe, G.

CARR: Who is Allingham?

TZARA: "Up the airy mountain, down the rushy glen, we daren't go a-hunting for fear of little men . . ." Cecily would regard any poem that came out of a hat with the gravest suspicion.

CARR: It is a librarian's duty to distinguish between poetry and a sort of belle-litter.

TZARA: Hello—why the extra cup?—why cucumber sandwiches? Who's coming to tea?

CARR: It is merely set for Gwendolen—she usually returns at about this hour.

TZARA: How perfectly delightful, and to be honest not unexpected. I am in love with Gwendolen and have come expressly to propose to her.

CARR: Well, that is a surprise.

TZARA: Surely not, Henry; I have made my feelings for Gwendolen quite plain.

CARR: Of course you have, my dear fellow. The way you pass her the cucumber sandwiches puts me in mind of nothing so much as a curate assisting at his first Holy Communion. But my surprise stems from the fact that you must surely have met Gwendolen at the Public Library, for she has left here every morning this week saying that that is where she is going, and Gwendolen is a scrupulously truthful girl. In fact, as her elder brother I have had to speak to her about it. Unrelieved truthfulness can give a young girl a reputation for insincerity. I have known plain girls with nothing to hide captivate the London season purely by discriminate mendacity.

TZARA: Oh, I assure you Gwendolen has been in the Public Library. But I have had to admire her from afar, all the way from Economics to Foreign Literature.

CARR: I had no idea Gwendolen knew any foreign languages, and I am not sure that I approve. It's the sort of thing that can only broaden a girl's mind.

TZARA: Well, in this library Foreign Literature includes English.

CARR: What a novel arrangement. Is any reason given?

TZARA (*impatiently*): The point is, Henry, I can't get to speak to her alone.

CARR: Ah, yes—her chaperone.

TZARA: Chaperone?

CARR: Yes—you don't imagine I'd let my sister go unchaperoned in a city largely frequented by foreigners. Gwendolen has made a friend in Zurich. I have not met her but

Gwendolen assures me that they are continuously in each other's company, and from a description which I have elicited by discreet questioning she cannot but be a wholesome and restraining influence, being practically middle-aged, plainly dressed, bespectacled and answering to the name of Joyce, oh good heavens. Is he after her money?

TZARA: Only in derisory instalments. He claims to be writing a novel, and has made a disciple out of Gwendolen. She transcribes for him, looks things up in works of reference, and so on. The poor girl is so innocent she does not stop to wonder what possible book could be derived from reference to Homer's *Odyssey* and the Dublin Street Directory for 1904.

CARR: Homer's *Odyssey* and the Dublin Street Directory?

TZARA: For 1904.

CARR: I admit it's an unusual combination of sources, but not wholly without possibilities. Anyway, there's no need to behave as though you were married to her already. You are not married to her already, and I don't think you ever will be.

TZARA: Why on earth do you say that?

CARR: In the first place, girls never marry Rumanians, and in the second place I don't give my consent.

TZARA: Your consent!

CARR: My dear fellow, Gwendolen is my sister and before I allow you to marry her you will have to clear up the whole question of Jack.

TZARA: Jack! What on earth do you mean? What do you mean, Henry, by Jack? I don't know anyone of the name of Jack.

CARR (*taking a library ticket from his pocket*): You left this here the last time you dined.

TZARA: Do you mean to say you have had my library ticket all this time? I had to pay a small fine in replacing it.

CARR: That was extravagant of you, since the ticket does not belong to you. It is made out in the name of Mr. Jack Tzara, and your name isn't Jack, it's Tristan.

TZARA: No, it isn't, it's Jack.

CARR: You have always told me it was Tristan. I have introduced
you to everyone as Tristan. You answer to the name of
Tristan. Your notoriety at the Meierei Bar is firmly
associated with the name Tristan. It is perfectly absurd
saying your name isn't Tristan.

TZARA: Well, my name is Tristan in the Meierei Bar and Jack
in the library, and the ticket was issued in the library.

CARR: To write—or at any rate to draw words out of a hat—
under one name, and appear at the Public Library under
another is an understandable precaution—but I cannot
believe that that is the whole explanation.

TZARA: My dear Henry, the explanation is perfectly simple.
One day last year, not long after the triumph at the
Meierei Bar of our noise concert for siren, rattle and fire-
extinguisher, I met Ulyanov, also known as Lenin, at the
Café Zum Adler with a group of Zimmerwaldists.

CARR: That sounds like the last word in revolutionary politics.
What does it mean?

TZARA: It describes those Socialists who at the Zimmerwald
Conference in 1915 called on the workers of the world to
oppose the war. Well, at the Zum Adler Lenin was raging
away against the chauvinist moderates who didn't necessarily
want to bayonet every man over the rank of NCO, when
someone at the bar piano started to play a Beethoven sonata.
Lenin went completely to pieces and when he recovered he
dried his eyes and lashed into the Dadaists, if you please.
Well, as a Dadaist myself I am the natural enemy of
bourgeois art and the natural ally of the political left, but
the odd thing about revolution is that the further left you go
politically the more bourgeois they like their art. Fortunately
at the Zum Adler my name meant nothing to Lenin, but a
few days later I met him at the library and he introduced
me to Cecily. "Tzara!" said she. "Not the Dadaist, I
hope!" "My younger brother, Tristan," I replied. "Most
unfortunate. Terrible blow to the family." When I filled up
my application form, for some reason the first name I
thought of was Jack. It has really turned out rather well.

CARR (*with great interest*): Cecily knows *Lenin*, does she?

TZARA: Oh, yes, he's made quite a disciple out of Cecily. She's helping him with his book on Imperialism.

CARR (*thoughtfully*): Did you say the reference section?

TZARA: They agree on everything, including art. It *is* odd, isn't it? I mean it is *the* contradiction of the radical movement.

CARR: There is nothing contradictory about it . . . Revolution in art is in no way connected with *class* revolution. Artists are members of a privileged class. Art is absurdly overrated by artists, which is understandable, but what is strange is that it is absurdly overrated by everyone else.

TZARA: Because man cannot live by bread alone.

CARR: Yes, he can. It's *art* he can't live on. "Bread—Peace— Freedom"—that's the slogan of revolution, I believe. What possible connection could there be between *that* and the shrill self-enclosed squabbles of rival ego-maniacs—formless painters, senseless poets, hatless sculptors——

TZARA (*coldly*): You are insulting me and my comrades in the Dada Exhibition——

CARR: —and exhibitionists in general. When I was at school, on certain afternoons we all had to do what was called Labour—weeding, sweeping, sawing logs for the boiler-room, that kind of thing; but if you had a chit from Matron you were let off to spend the afternoon messing about in the Art Room. Labour or Art. And you've got a chit for *life*? (*passionately*) *Where did you get it?* What is an artist? For every thousand people there's nine hundred doing the work, ninety doing well, nine doing good, and one lucky bastard who's the artist.

TZARA (*hard*): Yes, by Christ!—and when you see the drawings he made on the walls of the cave, and the fingernail patterns he one day pressed into the clay of the cooking pot, *then* you say, *My God, I am of these people!* It's not the hunters and the warriors that put you on the first rung of the ladder to consecutive thought and a rather unusual flair in your poncey trousers.

CARR: Oh yes it was. The hunter decorated the pot, the warrior scrawled the antelope on the wall, the artist came home with the kill. All of a piece. The idea of the artist as a special kind of human being is art's greatest achievement, and it's a fake!

TZARA: My God, you bloody English philistine—you ignorant smart-arse bogus bourgeois Anglo-Saxon prick! When the strongest began to fight for the tribe, and the fastest to hunt, it was the artist who became the priest-guardian of the magic that conjured the intelligence out of the appetites. Without him, man would be a coffee-mill. Eat—grind—shit. Hunt—*eat*—fight—*grind*—saw the logs—*shit*. The difference between being a man and being a coffee-mill is art. But that difference has become smaller and smaller and smaller. Art created patrons and was corrupted. It began to celebrate the ambitions and acquisitions of the pay-master. The artist has negated himself: paint—*eat*—sculpt—grind—write—*shit*.

(*A light change.*)

Without art man was a coffee-mill: but *with* art, man—is a coffee-mill! That is the message of Dada. —dada dada dada dada dada dada dada dada dada dada dada dada dada dada . . .

(TZARA *is shouting, raving.* CARR *immobile.*)

(*Normal light as* BENNETT *opens the door. Everything back to "normal".*)

BENNETT: Miss Gwendolen and Mr. Joyce.

(GWENDOLEN *and* JOYCE *appear as before.* BENNETT *retires.*)

JOYCE: Good morning, my name is James Joyce——

CARR: James Augusta?

JOYCE (*taken aback*): Was that a shot in the dark?

CARR: Not at all—I am a student of footnotes to expatriate Irish literature.

JOYCE: You know my work?

CARR: No—only your name.

TZARA: Miss Carr . . .

GWEN: Mr. Tzara . . .

CARR: . . . but something about you suggests Limerick.

JOYCE: Dublin, don't tell me you know it?

CARR: Only from the guidebook, and I gather you are in the process of revising that.

47

JOYCE: Yes.

GWEN: Oh! I'm sorry—how terribly rude! Henry—Mr. Joyce——

CARR: How'dyou do?

JOYCE: Delighted.

TZARA: Good day.

JOYCE: I just wanted to say——

GWEN: Do you know Mr. Tzara, the poet?

JOYCE: By sight, and reputation; but I am a martyr to
glaucoma and inflation. Recently as I was walking down the
Bahnhofstrasse my eye was caught by a gallery showcase
and I was made almost insensible with pain.

GWEN: Mr. Joyce has written a poem about it. It is something
you two have in common.

JOYCE: Hardly. Mr. Tzara's disability is monocular, and, by
rumour, affected, whereas I have certificates for conjunctivitis,
iritis and synechia, and am something of an international
eyesore.

GWEN: I mean poetry. I was thinking of your poem
"Bahnhofstrasse", beginning
   "The eyes that mock me sign the way
   Whereto I pass at eve of day,
   Grey way whose violet signals are
   The trysting and the twining star."

TZARA (to JOYCE): For your masterpiece
   I have great expectorations
   (GWEN's *squeak, "Oh!"*)
   For you I would eructate a monument.
   (*Oh!*)
   Art for art's sake—I defecate!

GWEN: Delectate . . .

TZARA: I'm a foreigner.

JOYCE: So am I.

GWEN: But it is the most beautiful thing I've ever heard. I have
a good ear, would you not agree, Mr. Tzara?

TZARA: It is the most perfect thing about you, Miss Carr.

GWEN: Oh, I hope not. That would leave no room for
development.

JOYCE: But have you not read any of Mr. Tzara's poems?

GWEN: To my shame I have not—but perhaps the shame is yours, Mr. Tzara.

TZARA: I accept it—but the matter can be easily put right, and at once.

GWEN (*fluttering*): Oh, Mr. Tzara! . . .

(TZARA *retires to the sideboard, or writing table if there is one, and begins to write fluently on a large piece of white paper.*)

CARR (*to* JOYCE): And what about you, Doris?

JOYCE: Joyce.

CARR: Joyce.

JOYCE: It is not as a poet that I come to see you, sir, but as the business manager of the English Players, a theatrical troupe.

CARR: The business manager?

JOYCE: Yes.

CARR: Well, if it's money you want, I'm afraid . . .

GWEN: Oh, Henry!—he's mounting a play, and he thought your official support——

JOYCE: Perhaps I'd better explain. It seems, sir, that my name is in bad odour among the British community in Zurich. Whether it is my occasional contribution to the neutralist press, or whether it is my version of *Mr. Dooley,* beginning:

"Who is the man, when all the gallant nations run to war,
Goes home to have his dinner by the very first cable car,
And as he eats his canteloupe contorts himself with mirth
To read the blatant bulletins of the rules of the earth?"

—and continuing:

"Who is the furious fellow who declines to go to church
Since pope and priest and parson left the poor man in
       the lurch
And taught their flocks the only way to save all human
       souls
Was piercing human bodies through with dum-dum
       bullet holes?"

—and proceeding to:

"Who is the tranquil gentleman who won't salute the
       State?
Or serve Nebuchadnezzar or proletariat

But thinks that every son of man has quite enough to do
To paddle down the stream of life his personal canoe?"
—by way of:
"Who is the meek philosopher who doesn't care a damn
About the yellow peril or the problem of Siam
And disbelieves that British Tar is water from life's fount
And will not gulp the Gospel of the German on the
                                                    Mount"
—and ending:
"It's Mr. Dooley
Mr. Dooley
The wisest wight our country ever knew!
'Poor Europe ambles
like sheep to shambles'
Sighs Mr. Dooley-ooley-ooley-ooo."
or some other cause altogether, the impression remains that
I regard both sides with equal indifference.

CARR: And you don't?

JOYCE: Only as an artist. As an artist, naturally I attach no
importance to the swings and roundabout of political history.
But I come here not as an artist but as James A. Joyce.
I am an Irishman. The proudest boast of an Irishman is—
I paid back my way . . .

CARR: So it is money.

JOYCE: A couple of pounds would be welcome—certainly, but
it is to repay a debt that I have come. Not long ago, after
many years of self-reliance and hardship during which my
work had been neglected and reviled even to the point of
being burned by a bigoted Dublin printer, there being no
other kind of printer available in Dublin, I received £100
from the Civil List at the discretion of the Prime Minister.

CARR: The Prime Minister——?

JOYCE: Mr. Asquith.

CARR: I am perfectly well aware who the Prime Minister *is*—
I am the representative of His Majesty's Government in
Zurich.

JOYCE: The Prime Minister is Mr. Lloyd George, but at that
time it was Mr. Asquith.

CARR: Oh yes.

JOYCE: I do not at this moment possess £100, nor was it the intention that I would repay the debt in kind. However I mentioned the English Players. By the fortune of war, Zurich has become the theatrical centre of Europe. Here culture is the continuation of war by other means—Italian opera against French painting—German music against Russian ballet—but nothing from England. Night after night, actors totter about the raked stages of this alpine renaissance, speaking in every tongue but one—the tongue of Shakespeare—of Sheridan—of Wilde . . . The English Players intend to mount a repertoire of masterpieces that will show the Swiss who leads the world in dramatic art.

CARR: Gilbert and Sullivan—by God!

GWEN: And also Mr. Joyce's own play *Exiles* which so far, unfortunately——

JOYCE: That's quite by the way——

CARR: *Patience!*

JOYCE: Exactly. First things first.

CARR: *Trial by Jury! Pirates of Penzance!*

JOYCE: We intend to begin with that quintessential English jewel, *The Importance of Being Earnest.*

CARR (*pause*): I don't know it. But I've heard of it and I don't like it. It is a play written by an Irish—(*glances at* GWENDOLEN) Gomorrahist—Now look here, Janice, I may as well tell you, His Majesty's Government——

JOYCE: I have come to ask you to play the leading role.

CARR: What?

JOYCE: We would be honoured and grateful.

CARR: What on earth makes you think that I am qualified to play the leading role in *The Importance of Being Earnest*?

GWEN: It was my suggestion, Henry. You were a wonderful Goneril at Eton.

CARR: Yes, I know, but——

JOYCE: We are short of a good actor to play the lead—he's an articulate and witty English gentleman——

CARR: Ernest?

JOYCE: Not Ernest—the other one.

CARR (*tempted*): No—no—I absolutely——

JOYCE: Aristocratic—romantic—epigrammatic—he's a young swell.

CARR: A swell . . . ?

JOYCE: He says things like, I may occasionally be a little overdressed but I make up for it by being immensely over-educated. That gives you the general idea of him.

CARR: How many changes of costume?

JOYCE: Two complete outfits.

CARR: Town or country?

JOYCE: First one then the other.

CARR: Indoors or out?

JOYCE: Both.

CARR: Summer or winter?

JOYCE: Summer but not too hot.

CARR: Not raining?

JOYCE: Not a cloud in the sky.

CARR: But he could be wearing—a boater?

JOYCE: It is expressly stipulated.

CARR: And he's not in—pyjamas?

JOYCE: Expressly proscribed.

CARR: Or in mourning?

JOYCE: Not the other one—Ernest.

CARR (*claps his hands once*): Describe the play briefly, omitting all but essential detail.

JOYCE: The curtain rises. A flat in Mayfair. Teatime. You enter in a bottle-green velvet smoking jacket with black frogging—hose white, cravat perfect, boots elastic-sided, trousers of your own choice.

CARR: I shall have to make certain expenditures.

JOYCE: Act Two. A rose garden. After lunch. Some by-play among the small parts. You enter in a debonair garden party outfit—beribboned boater, gaily striped blazer, parti-coloured shoes, trousers of your own choice.

CARR (*instantly*): Cream flannel.

JOYCE: Act Three. The morning room. A few moments later.

CARR: A change of costume?

JOYCE: Possibly by the alteration of a mere line or two of

dialogue . . .

CARR: You have brought a copy of the play?

JOYCE: I have it here.

CARR: Then let us retire to the next room and peruse it.

(CARR *opens the door of "his" room for* JOYCE.)

JOYCE: About those two pounds——

CARR (*generously, reaching for his wallet*): My dear Phyllis . . . !

(*—and closes it after them.*)

(*Pause. Freeze.*)

GWEN (*absently*): Gomorrahist . . . Silly bugger.

(TZARA *comes forward with rare diffidence, holding a hat like a brimming bowl. It transpires that he has written down a Shakespeare sonnet and cut it up into single words which he has placed in the hat.*)

TZARA: Miss Carr . . .

GWEN: Mr. Tzara!—you're not leaving? (*the hat*)

TZARA: Not before I offer you my poem.

(*He offers the hat.* GWEN *looks into it.*)

GWEN: Your technique is unusual.

TZARA: All poetry is a reshuffling of a pack of picture cards, and all poets are cheats. I offer you a Shakespeare sonnet, but it is no longer his. It comes from the wellspring where my atoms are uniquely organised, and my signature is written in the hand of chance.

GWEN: Which sonnet—was it?

TZARA: The eighteenth.

GWEN (*sadly*): "Shall I compare thee to a summer's day . . ."

". . . Thou art more lovely and more temperate.
Rough winds do shake the darling buds of May
And summer's lease hath all too short a date.
Sometimes too hot the eye of heaven shines,
And often is his gold complexion dimm'd;
And every fair from fair sometime declines,
By chance or nature's changing course untrimm'd;
But thy eternal summer shall not fade
Nor lose possession of that fair thou owest;
Nor shall Death brag thou wander'st in his shade,
When in eternal lines to time thou growest:

> So long as men can breathe or eyes can see,
> So long lives this and this gives life to thee . . ."

You tear him for his bad verses?

(*She lets a handful of words fall from her fingers, back into the hat, and her sadness starts to give way to anger.*)

These are but wild and whirling words, my lord.

TZARA: Ay, Madam.

GWEN: Truly I wish the gods had made thee poetical.

TZARA: I do not know what poetical is. Is it honest in word and deed? Is it a true thing?

GWEN: Sure he that made us with such large discourse, looking before and after, gave us not *that* capability, *and* god-like reason to fust in us unused.

TZARA: I was not born under a rhyming planet. Those fellows of infinite tongue that can rhyme themselves into ladies' favours, they do reason themselves out again. And that would set my teeth nothing on edge—*nothing* so much as mincing poetry.

GWEN (*rising to his vicious edge*): Thy honesty and love doth mince *this* matter—Put your bonnet for his right use, 'tis for the head! (*sniffs away a tear*) I had rather than forty shilling my book of songs and sonnets here.

(*She has turned away. He approaches with his hat offered.*)

TZARA (*gently*): But since he died, and poet better prove,
his for his style you'll read, mine for my—love.

(GWEN *hesitates but then takes the first slip of paper out of the hat.*)

GWEN: "Darling".

(*She now continues, holding on to all the pieces of paper she takes out.*)

> shake thou thy gold buds
> the untrimm'd but short fair shade
> shines—
> see, this lovely hot possession growest
> so long
> by nature's course—
> so . . . long—heaven!

(*She gives a little shriek, using "heaven" and turns her back*

on the hat, taking a few steps away from TZARA, *who takes
out the next few words, lowering the temperature* . . .)

TZARA: and declines,
  summer changing, more temperate complexion . . .

GWEN (*still flustered*): Pray don't talk to me about the weather,
  Mr. Tzara. Whenever people talk to me about the weather
  I always feel quite certain that they mean something else.

TZARA (*coming to her*): I do mean something else, Miss Carr.
  Ever since I met you I have admired you.
  (*He drops his few papers into the hat, she does likewise with
  hers, he puts the hat aside.*)

GWEN: For me you have always had an irresistible fascination.
  Even before I met you I was far from indifferent to you.
  As you know I have been helping Mr. Joyce with his new
  book, which I am convinced is a work of genius, and I am
  determined to secure for him the universal recognition he
  deserves. But alas, in fashionable society a girl receives few
  opportunities for intellectual connections. When Henry
  told me that he had a friend who edited a magazine of all
  that is newest and best in literature, I knew I was destined
  to love you.
  (*She has the folder she acquired in the Prologue and gives it to*
  TZARA.)

TZARA (*amazed*): Do you really love me, Gwendolen?

GWEN: Passionately!

TZARA: Darling, you don't know how happy you've made me.

GWEN: My own Tristan!
  (*They embrace.*)

TZARA (*breaking off*): But you don't mean that you couldn't love
  me if I didn't share your regard for Mr. Joyce as an artist?

GWEN: But you do.

TZARA: Yes. I know I *do*, but supposing——
  (*She kisses him on the mouth.*)
  (*They embrace.* JOYCE *re-enters.*)

JOYCE: Rise, sir, from that semi-recumbent posture!
  (TZARA *and* GWEN *spring apart.* JOYCE *walks across to the main
  door, picking up his hat, opens the door, addresses* TZARA.)
  Your monocle is in the wrong eye.

(TZARA *has indeed placed his monocle in the wrong eye. He*
replaces it. JOYCE *has left on his line.*)

GWEN: I must tell Henry!

TZARA: Have you ever seen my magazine "Dada", darling?

GWEN: Never, da-da-darling!

(GWEN *kisses him and runs into Henry's room.*)
(TZARA *starts reading the manuscript in the folder.*)
(*The main door opens again and* JOYCE *re-enters, pausing in*
the threshold. He is covered from head to breast in little bits
of white paper, each bit bearing one of the words of
Shakespeare's eighteenth sonnet, i.e. TZARA *was using Joyce's*
hat. The effect must be immediate and self-evident, and it is
probably necessary for the actor playing Joyce to change into
a specially prepared jacket and even a duplicate wig; the bits
of paper must be lightly stuck on to the hair and jacket,
for the play's need of them is not finished.)

JOYCE: What is the meaning of this?

TZARA: It has no meaning. It is without meaning as Nature is.
It is Dada.

JOYCE: Give further examples of Dada.

TZARA: The Zoological Gardens after closing time. The logical
gardenia. The bankrupt gambler. The successful gambler.
The Eggboard, a sport or pastime for the top ten thousand
in which the players, covered from head to foot in eggyolk,
leave the field of play.

JOYCE: Are you the inventor of this sport or pastime?

TZARA: I am not.

JOYCE: What is the name of the inventor?

TZARA: Arp.

JOYCE: Is he your sworn enemy, pet aversion, bête noir, or
otherwise persona non grata?

TZARA: He is not.

JOYCE: Is he your friend, comrade-in-arms, trusted confidant
or otherwise pal, mate or crony?

TZARA: He is.

JOYCE: By what familiarity, indicating possession and amicability
in equal parts, do you habitually refer to him?

TZARA: My friend Arp.

JOYCE: Alternating with what colloquialism redolent of virtue and longevity?

TZARA: Good old Arp.

JOYCE: Grasping any opportunity for paradox as might occur, in what way is the first name of your friend Arp singular?

TZARA: In that it is duplicate.

JOYCE: Namely?

TZARA: Hans Arp. Jean Arp.

JOYCE: How can this contradiction of two distinct and equal first names be accounted for?

TZARA: Linguistically, each being a translation of the other, from German into French and conversely.

JOYCE: Given a superficial knowledge of your friend's birth and parentage on the one hand, and of the political history of nineteenth-century Europe on the other, how would his bi-lingual nomination strike one?

TZARA: As understandable.

JOYCE: Why?

TZARA: He is a native of Alsace, of French background, and a German citizen by virtue of the conquest of 1870.

JOYCE: What declaration of an international and belligerent nature brought this ambivalence into sharp conflict?

TZARA: The declaration of war between Germany and France.

JOYCE: How did Hans or Jean Arp view the situation?

TZARA: As absurd.

JOYCE: How did he redress it?

TZARA: By making his way to Zurich and inventing the Egg-board, a sport or pastime for the top ten thousand in which the players, covered from head to foot in eggyolk, leave the field of play.

JOYCE: From whom did he receive encouragement and friend-ship?

TZARA: From Hugo Ball.

JOYCE: Describe Ball by epithet.

TZARA: Unspherical. Tall, thin, sacerdotal, German.

JOYCE: Describe him by enumeration of his occupations and preoccupations.

TZARA: Novelist, journalist, philosopher, poet, artist, mystic,

pacifist, founder of the Cabaret Voltaire at the Meierei
Bar, number one Spiegelgasse.

JOYCE: Did Ball keep a diary?

TZARA: He did.

JOYCE: Was it published?

TZARA: It was.

JOYCE: Is it in the public domain by virtue of the expiration of
copyright protection as defined in the Berne Convention
of 1886?

TZARA: It is not.

JOYCE: Quote judiciously so as to combine maximum information
with minimum liability.

TZARA: "I went to Herr Ephraim, the owner of the Meierei,
and said, 'Herr Ephraim, please let me have your room,
I want to start a nightclub.' Herr Ephraim agreed and gave
me the room. And I went to some people I knew and said,
'Please give me a picture. I should like to put on an
exhibition in my nightclub.' I went to the friendly Zurich
press and said, 'Put in some announcements. There is
going to be an international cabaret. We shall do great
things.' And they gave me pictures and they put in my
announcements."

JOYCE: On what date did the first announcement appear in the
Zurich press?

TZARA: On February 2nd, 1916.

JOYCE: Quote discriminately from Ball's diary in such a manner
as to avoid forfeiting the goodwill of his executors.

TZARA: "About six in the evening, when we were still hammering
and putting up Futurist posters, there appeared an
Oriental-looking deputation of four little men with port-
folios and pictures under their arms, bowing politely many
times. They introduced themselves: Marcel Janco the
painter, Tristan Tzara, Georges Janco, and a fourth whose
name I did not catch. Arp was also there, and we came to
an understanding without many words. Soon Janco's
opulent Archangels hung alongside the other objects of
beauty, and that same evening Tzara gave a reading of
poems, conservative in style, which he rather endearingly

58

fished out of the various pockets of his coat."

JOYCE: Is that the coat?

TZARA: It is.

JOYCE: In what regard is a coat inferior, and in what superior, to a hat in so far as they are interchangeable in the production of poetry?

TZARA: *Inferior* to a hat in regard to the tendency of one or both sleeves to hang down in front of the eyes, with the resultant possibility of the wearer falling off the edge of the platform. *Superior* to a hat in regard to the number of its pockets.

JOYCE: In so far as what technique were your poems on that historic occasion conservative?

TZARA: In so far as I produced each one entire and consecutive in its parts from one pocket, as opposed to producing it piecemeal and randomly from different pockets. Also in so far as I read only one poem at a time. Also in so far as I read it without accompaniment of whistles, rattles and percussion of packing cases.

JOYCE: Soon afterwards could this be said?

TZARA: It could not.

JOYCE: Corroborate discreetly from any contemporary diarist whose estate is not given to obsessive litigation over trivial infringements of copyright.

TZARA: "On February 26th Richard Huelsenbeck arrived from Berlin, and on March 30th we performed some stupendous Negro music. Herr Tristan Tzara was the initiator of a performance, the first in Zurich and in the world, of simultanist verse, including a poème simultané of his own composition."

JOYCE: Quote severally your recollections of what was declaimed synchronously.

TZARA: I began, "Boum boum boum il déshabille sa chair quand les grenouilles humides commencerent a brûler." Huelsenbeck began, "Ahoi ahoi des admirals gwirktes Beinkleid schnell zerfallt." Janco chanted, "I can hear the whip o' will around the hill and at five o'clock when tea is set I like to have my tea with some brunette, everybody's doing it, doing it." The title of the poem was "Admiral

Seeks House To Let".

JOYCE: Is it the case that within a remarkably short time performances of this kind made Dada in general and Tzara in particular names to conjure with wherever art was discussed?

TZARA: It is.

(*All this time, JOYCE has been picking bits of paper from his hair and from his clothes, replacing each bit in his hat, which is on his knees. Casually, on the word "conjure", he conjures from the hat a white carnation, apparently made from the bits of paper (he turns the hat up to show it is empty). He tosses the carnation at TZARA.*)

JOYCE: How would you describe this triumph?

TZARA (*putting the carnation into his buttonhole*): As just and proper. Well merited. An example of enterprise and charm receiving their due.

(*JOYCE starts to pull silk hankies from the hat.*)

JOYCE: Realising that this local bourgeois-baiting pussy-cat, Dada, had grown into a tiger standing for scandal, provocation and moral outrage through art, what, reduced to their simplest reciprocal form, were Tzara's thoughts about Ball's thoughts about Tzara, and Tzara's thoughts about Ball's thoughts about Tzara's thoughts about Ball?

TZARA: He thought that he thought that he would ride the tiger, whereas he knew that he knew that he knew that he would not.

JOYCE: And did they?

TZARA: They did and they didn't. Ball left Zurich, eventually became a Catholic and lived quietly among peasants until his death in 1927. Tzara remained to guide the Dada revolution into the next stage, Surrealism—but that was in Paris after the war.

JOYCE: What did Dada bring to pictorial art, sculpture, poetry and music that had not been brought to these activities previously in . . .

(*The appropriate flags start coming out of the hat.*)

. . . Barcelona, New York, Paris, Rome and St. Petersburg by, for example, Picabia, Duchamp, Satie, Marinetti, and

Mayakovsky who shouts his fractured lines in a yellow blazer with blue roses painted on his cheeks?

TZARA: The word Dada.

JOYCE: Describe sensibly without self-contradiction, and especially without reference to people stuffing bread rolls up their noses, how the word Dada was discovered.

TZARA: Tristan Tzara discovered the word Dada by accident in a Larousse Dictionary. It has been said, and he does not deny, that a paper-knife was inserted at random into the book. In French *dada* is a child's word for a hobbyhorse. In German it denotes a simple-minded preoccupation with babies. Huelsenbeck recounts how *he* discovered the word one day in Hugo Ball's French-German dictionary in Hugo Ball's room while Tzara was not present. Hans or Jean Arp, however, has stated, "I hereby declare that Tristan Tzara found the word Dada on February the 8th 1916 at six o'clock in the afternoon. I was present with my twelve children when Tzara first uttered the word which filled us with justified enthusiasm. This occurred in the Café de la Terrasse in Zurich and I was wearing a brioche in my left nostril."

JOYCE: Were there further disagreements between Tzara and Huelsenbeck?

TZARA: There were.

JOYCE: As to?

TZARA: As to the meaning and purpose of Dada.

JOYCE: As indicated?

TZARA: As indicated by manifestoes written by Tzara and those by Huelsenbeck.

JOYCE: Huelsenbeck demanding, for example?

TZARA: International revolutionary union of all creative men and women on the basis of radical Communism—expropriation of property—socialization . . .

JOYCE: As opposed to Tzara's demanding?

TZARA: The right to urinate in different colours.

JOYCE: Each person in different colours at different times, or different people in each colour all the time? Or everbody multi-coloured every time?

TZARA: It was more to make the point that making poetry
should be as natural as making water——
JOYCE (*rising: the conjuring is over*): God send you don't make
them in the one hat.
(*This is too much for* TZARA.)
TZARA: By God, you supercilious streak of Irish puke! You
four-eyed, bog-ignorant, potato-eating ponce! Your art
has failed. You've turned literature into a religion and
it's as dead as all the rest, it's an overripe corpse and you're
cutting fancy figures at the wake. It's too late for geniuses!
Now we need vandals and desecrators, simple-minded
demolition men to smash centuries of baroque subtlety, to
bring down the temple, and thus finally, to reconcile the
shame and the necessity of being an artist! Dada! *Dada!*
Dada!!
(*He starts to smash whatever crockery is to hand; which done,
he strikes a satisfied pose.* JOYCE *has not moved.*)
JOYCE: You are an over-excited little man, with a need for
self-expression far beyond the scope of your natural gifts.
This is not discreditable. Neither does it make you an
artist. An artist is the magician put among men to gratify—
capriciously—their urge for immortality. The temples are
built and brought down around him, continuously and
contiguously, from Troy to the fields of Flanders. If there
is any meaning in any of it, it is in what survives as art,
yes even in the celebration of tyrants, yes even in the
celebration of nonentities. What now of the Trojan War if
it had been passed over by the artist's touch? Dust. A
forgotten expedition prompted by Greek merchants looking
for new markets. A minor redistribution of broken pots.
But it is we who stand enriched, by a tale of heroes, of a
golden apple, a wooden horse, a face that launched a
thousand ships—and above all, of Ulysses, the wanderer,
the most human, the most complete of all heroes—husband,
father, son, lover, farmer, soldier, pacifist, politician, inventor
and adventurer . . . It is a theme so overwhelming that I
am almost afraid to treat it. And yet I with my Dublin
Odyssey will double that immortality, yes by God *there's*

a corpse that will dance for some time yet and *leave the world precisely as it finds it*—and if you hope to shame it into the grave with your fashionable magic, I would strongly advise you to try and acquire some genius and if possible some subtlety before the season is quite over. Top o' the morning, Mr. Tzara!

(*With which* JOYCE *produces a rabbit out of his hat, puts the hat on his head, and leaves, holding the rabbit.*)

(CARR's *voice is heard off.*)

CARR (*voice off*): "Really, if the lower orders don't set us a good example what on earth is the use of them? They seem as a class to have absolutely no sense of moral responsibility."

(TZARA *has moved to* CARR's *door. He opens it, and goes through.*)

(*voice off*) "How are you, my dear Ernest. What brings you up to town?"—"Pleasure, pleasure—eating as usual, I see, Algy . . ."

(CARR *enters, as Old Carr, holding a book.*)

Algy! The other one. Personal triumph in the demanding role of Algernon Montcrieff. The Theater zur Kaufleuten on Pelikanstrasse, an evening in Spring, the English Players in that quintessential English jewel "The Imprudence of Being—" Now I've forgotten the first one. By Oscar Wilde. Henry Carr as Algy. Other parts played by Tristan Rawson, Cecil Palmer, Ethel Turner, Evelyn Cotton . . . forget the rest. Tickets five francs, four bob a nob and every seat filled, must have made a packet for the Irish lout and his cronies— still, not one to bear a grudge, not after all these years, and him dead in the cemetery up the hill, unpleasant as it is to be dragged through the courts for a few francs—after I'd paid for my trousers *and* filled every seat in the house— *not* very pleasant to be handed ten francs like a *tip!*—and then asking me for twenty-five francs for tickets—bloody nerve—Here, I got it out——

(*From his pocket, a tattered document.*)

—Bezirksgericht Zuerich, Zurich District Court, Justices Billeter (presiding) and Hammann and Kaufmann (participating) in the case of Dr. James Joyce—doctor my eye—plaintiff and counter-defendant versus Henry Carr, defendant and counter-plaintiff, with reference to the claim for settlement of the following issues: (a) Suit: Is defendant and counter-plaintiff (that's me) obliged to pay the plaintiff and counter-defendant (that's him) twenty-five francs? (b) Counter-suit: is plaintiff and counter-defendant bound to pay defendant and counter-plaintiff four hundred and seventy-five francs, or possibly three hundred francs? Have you got that? Joyce says I owe him twenty-five francs for tickets. I say Joyce owes me four hundred and seventy-five francs as my share of the profits, or alternatively three hundred francs for the trousers, etcetera, purchased by me for my performance as Henry—or rather—*god dammit!*— the other one . . .

Incidentally, you may or may not have noticed that I got my wires crossed a bit here and there, you know how it is when the old think-box gets stuck in a groove and before you know where you are you've jumped the points and suddenly you think, No, steady on, old chap, that was Algernon—*Algernon!*—There you are—all coming back now, I've got it straight, I'll be all right from here on. In fact, anybody hanging on just for the cheap comedy of senile confusion might as well go because now I'm on to how I met Lenin and could have changed the course of history etcetera, what's this?? (*the document*) Oh yes.

Erkannt—has decided that. 1. Der Beklagte, the defendant, Henry Carr, is obliged to pay den Klager, the plaintiff, James Joyce, twenty-five francs. The counter-claim of Henry Carr is denied. Herr Carr to indemnify Doktor Joyce sixty francs for trouble and expenses. In other words, a travesty of justice. Later the other case came up—Oh yes, he sued me for slander, claimed I called him a swindler and a cad . . . Thrown out of court, naturally. But it was the money with Joyce. Well, it was a long time ago. He left Zurich after the war, went to Paris, stayed twenty years and turned up here again in December 1940. Another war . . . But he was a sick man then, perforated ulcer, and in January he was dead . . . buried one cold snowy day in the Fluntern

Cemetery up the hill.

I dreamed about him, dreamed I had him in the witness box, a masterly cross-examination, case practically won, admitted it all, the whole thing, the trousers, everything, and I *flung* at him—"And what did you do in the Great War?" "I wrote *Ulysses*," he said. "What did you do?"

Bloody nerve.

(BLACK OUT.)

ACT II

THE LIBRARY

The set however is not "lit" at the beginning of the Act.

Apart from the bookcases, etc. the Library's furniture includes CECILY's *desk, which is perhaps more like a counter forming three sides of a square.*

Most of the light is on CECILY *who stands patiently at the front of the stage, waiting for the last members of the audience to come in and sit down.*

The performance of the whole of this lecture is not a requirement, but is an option. After "To resume" it could pick up at any point, e.g. "Lenin was convinced . . ." or "Karl Marx had taken it as an axiom . . ."; but no later than that.

CECILY'S LECTURE

To resume.

It was with considerable surprise that Marx learned of the Russian translation of *Das Kapital*. This appeared in St. Petersburg in 1872, before being translated into any other language. He didn't know what to make of it. The conditions for a socialist revolution as he saw it did not exist in Russia at all. Two thirds of the population were peasants, the industrial age had hardly begun, and the proletariat was correspondingly insignificant. According to Marxist theory Russia still had to pass through the whole bourgeois-capitalist cycle.

But there were also good reasons for Russians to read Marx. Some believed that Russia would find a short cut to

66

the Communist society through a peasant revolution.
Others were content to adopt Communist ideals for the
Populist movement, which was the main revolutionary
movement of the time. The Populists—the Narodniki—
hoped, through education or incitement—to get the weight
of those millions of peasants behind the wheel of reform.
But the freedom of action and expression which had long
been won in Western Europe simply did not exist in Russia,
and by 1874 Populist activity had been crushed. As a result,
some of the Narodniki formed a secret party named "Land
and Freedom". But the party soon split over the question
of violence. Plekhanov, the leading Russian Marxist, took
his supporters out of the party. The remainder, now calling
themselves "The People's Will", dedicated themselves to
terrorism, with the assassination of the Tsar, Alexander II,
as their main objective. This they achieved in March, 1881.
The leaders of the People's Will were all caught, and hanged.
Plekhanov left Russia and settled in Switzerland. Here in
exile, he and his associates laid the foundations of the
Russian Worker's Party which evolved into the Communist
Party.

The leader of the assassins had said that history sometimes needed a push. Marx held that terrorism was
unscientific and useless. Events after 1881 supported Marx.
Alexander II had freed the serfs and allowed modest
reforms, but with his death repression came down more
tightly than ever. The reforms had evidently been a mistake.
Alexander III set out to re-Russianise Russia. Six years
later there was a last flicker from the party of the People's
Will. A group of students were arrested while plotting to
kill the Tsar.

Among them was the eldest son of an uncontroversial
family living in Simbirsk—Alexander Ulyanov, the 20
year old brother of Vladimir. The family knew nothing of
his activities, and were shocked by his arrest. Vladimir was
nearly seventeen. The father, a district inspector of schools,
had died the previous year. When news of the arrest
reached Simbirsk, the mother set out on the thousand mile

journey to St. Petersburg to plead for Alexander's life. One day in May when she had visited him in prison the night before, she learned from a newspaper bought in the street that Alexander had been hanged.

Vladimir was preparing at this time for his final examinations at high school. He came out top. The family moved to Kazan where Vladimir entered the university, and it was in Kazan, studying in the back kitchen in the Ulyanov apartment just outside this ancient Eastern city, that Vladimir first read Marx. His fidelity to Marx was established then and it never wavered. Marx had shown the only way forward. To quote Marx was enough to settle an argument. To question Marx was to betray the revolution.

Vladimir's role as the public conscience of Marxist orthodoxy began when he was in Siberian exile in the late 1890s—his arrest in 1895 had followed his first trip abroad to establish relations with Plekhanov and other Russian Marxists exiled in Geneva. During his own exile in Siberia, Vladimir began signing his articles with the *nom de guerre* "Lenin".

By this time he had been joined by a comrade, Nadezhda Krupskaya, whom he married in exile.

Lenin was convinced, like Marx, that history worked dialectically, that it advanced through the clash of opposing forces and not through the pragmatic negotiation of stiles and stepping-stones. He was a hard-liner. The class war was war, and to direct it effectively the Party had to be a compact group of professional revolutionaries who gave the orders. Out of one exile and into another, self-imposed outside Russia, Lenin encountered opposition in the party. Many of his colleagues wanted a more diffuse party, reaching down to the factory floor. Lenin answered that in the Russian autocracy this was useless and harmful. So there was a crack in the party façade, and in 1903 at the Second Congress, in the August heat of the Tottenham Court Road in London, it split the party down the middle. The issue finally revolved on the control of the party newspaper. In an atmosphere of strained friendships and bitter recriminations, Lenin got his majority. From then on, his faction of the Russian Social Democratic Labour Party was known as the "majoritarians"—the Bolsheviki.

But the vote in Congress turned out to be a hollow victory. Within months the Bolsheviks were ironically named. The Congress minority—the Mensheviks—regained control of the party paper and of the Central Committee, and made a much stronger impression during the abortive 1905 revolution in St. Petersburg. When the revolution failed, the Mensheviks retreated into the shell of semi-legal Marxism: the Revisionists were in the citadel. But Lenin had already left it, taking the grail with him, and for ten more years in exile he waged a war of words against all revisionists and reformists. And in 1914 the war produced a new enemy of Marxism—the patriot.

Karl Marx had taken it as an axiom that the workers of different countries had more in common with each other than with their bourgeois compatriots. At conference after conference right up to the eve of hostilities, socialists resolved to have no part of a capitalist war. But in August 1914 war fever swept over the socialist movement. In the Reichstag the Social Democrats voted almost to a man in favour of war credits. Against them, Russian Social Democrats also discovered that they were first and foremost patriots—or as Lenin now called them, Social Chauvinists.

The war caught Lenin and his wife in Galicia, in Austro-Hungary. After a brief internment they got into Switzerland and settled in Berne. In 1916, needing a better library than the one in Berne, Lenin came to Zurich . . . (THE LIBRARY SET IS NOW LIT.)

. . intending to stay two weeks. But he and Nadezhda liked it here and decided to stay. They rented a room in the house of a shoe-maker named Kammerer at 14 Spiegelgasse. Zurich during the war was a magnet for refugees, exiles, spies, anarchists, artists and radicals of all kinds. Here could be seen James Joyce, reshaping the novel into the permanent form of his own monument, the book the world now knows as *Ulysses!*—and here, too, the Dadaists were

performing nightly at the Cabaret Voltaire in the Meierei
Bar at Number One Spiegelgasse, led by a dark, boyish
and obscure Rumanian poet . . .

(JOYCE *is seen passing among the bookshelves; and also* CARR,
*now monocled and wearing blazer, cream flannels, boater . . .
and holding a large pair of scissors which he snips speculatively
as he passes between the bookcases.* JOYCE *and* CARR *pass out
of view.*)

Every morning at nine o'clock when the library opened,
Lenin would arrive.

(LENIN *arrives, saying "Good morning", in Russian:
"Zdvasvitsa".*)

He would work till the lunch hour, when the library
closed, and then return and work until six, except on
Thursdays when we remained closed. He was working on
his book on Imperialism.

(LENIN *is at work among books and papers.*)

On January 22nd, 1917, at the Zurich People's House
Lenin told an audience of young people, "We of the older
generation may not live to see the decisive battles of the
coming revolution." We all believed that that was so. But
one day hardly more than a month later, a Polish comrade,
Bronsky, ran into the Ulyanov house with the news that
there was a revolution in Russia . . .

(NADYA *enters as in the Prologue, and she and* LENIN *repeat
the Russian conversation previously enacted. This time*
CECILY *translates it for the audience, pedantically repeating
each speech in English, even the simple "No!" and "Yes!"
The* LENINS *leave.* NADYA *says "Das vedanya" to* CECILY
(*i.e. Goodbye*) *as she goes.*)

As Nadezhda writes in her *Memories of Lenin* "From the
moment the news of the February revolution came, Ilyich
burned with eagerness to go to Russia." But this was easier
said than done, in this landlocked country. Russia was at
war with Germany. And Lenin was no friend of the Allied
countries. His war policy made him a positive danger to
them;

(CARR *enters, very debonair in his boater and blazer, etc.* CARR

has come to the library as a "spy", and his manner betrays
this until CECILY *addresses him.*)
indeed it was clear that the British and the French would
wish to prevent Lenin from leaving Switzerland. And that
they would have him watched. Oh!
(CECILY *sees* CARR *who hands her the visiting card he*
received from BENNETT *in Act One.*)

CECILY: Tristan Tzara. Dada, Dada, Dada . . . *Why, it's Jack's*
younger brother!!

CARR: You must be Cecily!

CECILY: Ssssh!

CARR: You are!

CECILY: And you, I see from your calling card, are Jack's
decadent nihilist younger brother.

CARR: Oh, I'm not really a decadent nihilist at all, Cecily. You
mustn't think that I am a decadent nihilist.

CECILY: If you are not then you have certainly been deceiving us
all in a very inexcusable manner. To *masquerade* as a
decadent nihilist—or at any rate to ruminate in different
colours and display the results in the Bahnhofstrasse—
would be hypocritical.

CARR (*taken aback*): Oh! Of course, I have been rather *louche*
and devil-take-the-hindmost.

CECILY: I am glad to hear it.

CARR: In fact now you mention the subject I have made quite
a corner in voluptuous disdain.

CECILY: I don't think you should be so proud of it, however
pleasant it must be. You have been a great disappointment
to your brother.

CARR: Well, my brother has been a great disappointment to me,
and to Dada. His mother isn't exactly mad about him
either. My brother Jack is a booby, and if you want to
know why he is a booby, I will tell you why he is a booby.
He told me that you were rather pretty, whereas you are at
a glance the prettiest girl in the whole world. Have you got
any books here one can borrow?

CECILY: I don't think you ought to talk to me like that during
library hours. However, as the reference section is about to

71

close for lunch I will overlook it. Intellectual curiosity is not so common that one can afford to discourage it. What kind of books were you wanting?

CARR: Any kind at all.

CECILY: Is there no limit to the scope of your interests?

CARR: It is rather that I wish to increase it. An overly methodical education has left me to fend as best I can with some small knowledge of the aardvark, a mastery of the abacus and a facility for abstract art. An aardvark, by the way, is a sort of African pig found mainly——

CECILY: I know only too well what an aardvark is, Mr. Tzara. To be frank, you strike a sympathetic chord in me.

CARR: Politically, I haven't really got beyond anarchism.

CECILY: I see. Your elder brother, meanwhile——

CARR: Bolshevism. And you, I suppose . . . ?

CECILY: Zimmervaldism!

CARR: Oh, Cecily, will you not make it your mission to reform me? We can begin over lunch. It will give me an appetite. Nothing gives me an appetite so much as renouncing my beliefs over a glass of hock.

CECILY: I'm afraid I am too busy to reform you today. I must spend the lunch hour preparing references for Lenin.

CARR: Some faithful governess seeking fresh pastures?

CECILY: Far from it. I refer to Vladimir Ilyich who with my little help is writing his book on "Imperialism, the highest stage of capitalism".

CARR: Of course—*Lenin*. But surely, now that the revolution has broken out in St. Petersburg, he will be anxious to return home.

CECILY: That is true. When the history of the Revolution—or indeed of anything else—is written, Switzerland is unlikely to loom large in the story. However, all avenues are closed to him. He will have to travel in disguise with false papers. Oh, but I fear I have said too much already. Vladimir is positive that there are agents watching him and trying to ingratiate themselves with those who are close to him. The British are among the most determined, though the least competent. Only yesterday the Ambassador received secret instructions to watch the ports.

CARR (*ashamed*): The ports?

CECILY: At the same time, the Consul in Zurich has received a flurry of cryptic telegrams suggesting intense and dramatic activity—"Knock 'em cold"—"Drive 'em Wilde"—"Break a leg"—and one from the Ambassador himself, "Thinking of you tonight, Horace."

CARR: I think I can throw some light on that. The Consul has been busy for several weeks in rehearsals which culminated last evening in a performance at the Theater zur Kaufleuten on Pelikanstrasse. I happened to be present.

CECILY: That would no doubt explain why he virtually left the Consulate's affairs in the hands of his manservant—who, fortunately, has radical sympathies.

CARR: Good heavens!

CECILY: You seem surprised.

CARR: Not at all. I have a servant myself.

CECILY: I am afraid that I disapprove of servants.

CARR: You are quite right to do so. Most of them are without scruples.

CECILY: In the socialist future, no one will have any.

CARR: So I believe. To whom did this manservant pass the Consul's correspondence?

CECILY: Your brother Jack. Oh dear, there I go again! You are not a bit like your brother. You are more English.

CARR: I assure you I am as Bulgarian as he is.

CECILY: He is Rumanian.

CARR: They are the same place. Some people call it the one, some the other.

CECILY: I didn't know that, though I always suspected it.

CARR: Anyway, now that *Earnest* has opened, no doubt the Consul will relieve his servant of diplomatic business. In all fairness, he did have a personal triumph in a most demanding role.

CECILY: *Earnest*??

CARR: No—the other one.

CECILY: What do you mean by *Earnest*?

CARR: *The Importance of Being Earnest* by Oscar Wilde.

CECILY: I don't know it. But I've heard of it and I don't like it. It is a play written by an Irish-coxcomb and bugbear of the Home Rule sodality, so I hear.

CARR: Your ears deceive you. Far from being a bugbear of the Home Rule sodality, Cecily, Wilde was indifferent to politics. He may occasionally have been a little overdressed but he made up for it by being immensely uncommitted.

CECILY: That is my objection to him. The sole duty and justification for art is social criticism.

CARR: That is a most interesting view of the sole duty and justification for art, Cecily, but it has the disadvantage that a great deal of what we call art has no such function and yet in some way it gratifies a hunger that is common to princes and peasants.

CECILY: In an age when the difference between prince and peasant was thought to be in the stars, Mr. Tzara, art was naturally an affirmation for the one and a consolation to the other; but we live in an age when the social order is seen to be the work of material forces and we have been given an entirely new kind of responsibility, the responsibility of changing society.

CARR: No, no, no, no, no—my dear girl!—art doesn't change society, it is merely changed by it.

(*From here the argument becomes gradually heated.*)

CECILY: Art *is* society! It is one part of many parts all touching each other, everything from poetry to politics. And until the whole is reformed, artistic decadence, whether in the form of the perfectly phrased epigram or a hatful of words flung in the public's face, is a luxury which only artists can afford.

CARR: Kindly do not confuse a Dada raffle with Victorian high comedy——

CECILY: Both bourgeois—both decadent——

CARR: You are familiar with neither——

CECILY: Art is a critique of society or it is nothing!

CARR: Do you know Gilbert and Sullivan??!

CECILY: I know Gilbert but not Sullivan.

CARR: Well, if you knew Iolanthe like I know Iolanthe——

CECILY: I doubt it——

CARR: Patience!

CECILY: How dare you!

CARR: Pirates! Pinafore!

CECILY: Control yourself!

CARR: *Ruddigore!*

CECILY: This is a Public Library, Mr. Tzara!

CARR: *GONDOLIERS, Madam!*

(*Another "time slip . . ."*)

CECILY: I don't think you ought to talk to me like that during library hours. However as the reference section is about to close for lunch I will overlook it. Intellectual curiosity is not so common that one can afford to discourage it. What kind of books were you wanting?

CARR: Any kind at all. You choose. I should like you, if you would, to make it your mission to reform me. We can begin over lunch.

CECILY: I'm afraid I am too busy to reform you today. You will have to reform yourself. Here is an article which I have been translating for Vladimir Ilyich. It is addressed to the British, French and German Socialists who have deserted the correct path for economism, opportunism and social chauvinism.

(*She hands him the folder which came into her possession in the Prologue. It is identical to the one given by* GWEN *to* TZARA.)

CARR: That sounds awfully serious. What does it mean?

CECILY: Trade unions, parliament and support for the war. You may not be aware, Mr. Tzara, that in the governments of Western Europe today there are ten Socialist ministers.

CARR: I must admit my work has prevented me from taking an interest in European politics. But ten is certainly impressive.

CECILY: It is scandalous. They are supporting an imperialist war. To a socialist it makes no difference who wins: it is a war fought between slave-owners over a fairer distribution of slaves. Meanwhile the real struggle, the class war, is being undermined by these revisionists like Kautsky and MacDonald.

CARR (*puzzled*): Do you mean Ramsay MacDonald, Cecily?

CECILY: I don't mean Flora Macdonald, Mr. Tzara.

CARR: But he's an absolute Bolshie. Everybody knows that—he opposed the war.

CECILY: He is still an economist and opportunist.

CARR: But do you mean that forcing up wages and voting their own chaps into power is against the interests of the workers?

CECILY: Of course. It is working within the bourgeois capitalist system and postponing its destruction. Karl Marx has shown that capitalism is digging its own grave. Left to itself it will destroy itself. As the gap between rich and poor gets wider——

CARR: But it doesn't.

CECILY: Not at the moment, but Vladimir Ilyich has shown in his new book *Imperialism, the Highest Stage of Capitalism* that the European Worker is benefitting from the exploitation of his colonial brothers. Imperialism has introduced a breathing space, but the inexorable working-out of Marx's theory of capital——

CARR: No, no, no, no, my dear girl—Marx got it wrong. He got it wrong for good reasons but he got it wrong just the same. And twice over. In the first place he was the victim of an historical accident, and in the second place his materialism made a monkey out of him, and of his theory——

CECILY (*coldly*): Mr. Tzara, you are insulting me and my comrades——

CARR: —and especially of his comrades. The historical accident could have happened to anybody. By bad luck he encountered the capitalist system at its most deceptive period. The industrial revolution had crowded the people into slums and enslaved them in factories, but it had not yet begun to bring them the benefits of an industrialised society. Marx looked about him and saw that the system depended on a wretched army of wage slaves. He drew the lesson that the wealth of the capitalist was the counterpart to the poverty of the worker and had in fact been stolen from the worker in the form of unpaid labour. He thought that was how the whole thing worked. That false assumption was itself added to a false premise. This premise was that people were

76

a sensational kind of material object and would behave predictably in a material world. Marx predicted that they would behave according to their class. But they didn't. Deprived, self-interested, bitter or greedy as the case may be, they showed streaks of superior intelligence, superior strength, superior morality . . . Legislation, unions, share capital, consumer power—in all kinds of ways and for all kinds of reasons, the classes moved closer together instead of further apart. The critical moment never came. It receded. The tide must have turned at about the time when *Das Kapital* after eighteen years of hard labour was finally coming off the press, a moving reminder, Cecily, of the folly of authorship. How sweet you look suddenly—pink as a rose.

CECILY: That's because I'm about to puke into your nancy straw hat, you *prig*!—you swanking canting fop, you bourgeois intellectual humbugger, you—*artist*! Do you think that's what socialism is about?—being allowed to strike, to vote, to buy or not to buy, allowed this and allowed that?—*do you think it's about winning concessions?*—Socialism is about *ownership*—the natural right of the people to the common ownership of their country and its resources, the *land*, and what is *under* the land and what *grows* on the land, and all the profits and the benefits! A new society, root and branch, it won't grow like leaves on a tree. Marx warned us against the liberals, the philanthropists, the piecemeal reformers—change won't come from *them* but from a head-on collision, *that's* how history works! When Lenin was 21 there was famine in Russia. The intellectuals organised relief—soup kitchens, seed corn, all kinds of do-gooding with Tolstoy in the lead. Lenin did—nothing. He understood that the famine was a force for the revolution, that it would help to break down the peasantry and bring Russia closer to industrialised capitalism, closer to socialist revolution, closer to the dictatorship of the proletariat, closer to the Communist society. Twenty-one years old, in Samara, in 1890–91. He was a boy, and he understood that, so don't talk to me about superior morality, you patronising

77

Kant-struck prig, all the time you're talking about the classes you're trying to imagine how I'd looked stripped off to my knickers——

CARR: That's a lie!

(*But apparently it isn't. As* CECILY *continues to speak we get a partial Carr's-mind view of her. Coloured lights begin to play over her body, and most of the other light goes except for a bright spot on Carr. Faintly from 1974, comes the sound of the big band playing "The Stripper".* CARR *is in a trance. The music builds.* CECILY *might perhaps climb on to her desk. The desk may have "cabaret lights" built into it for use at this point.*)

CECILY: In England the rich own the poor and the men own the women. Five per cent of the people own eighty per cent of the property. The only way is the way of Marx, and of Lenin, the enemy of all revisionism—of economism—opportunism—liberalism—of bourgeois anarchist individualism—of quasi-socialist ad hoc-ism, of syndicalist quasi-Marxist populism—liberal quasi-communist opportunism, economist quasi-internationalist imperialism, social chauvinist quasi-Zimmervaldist Menshevism, self-determinist quasi-socialist annexationism, Kautskyism, Bundism, Kantism——

CARR: *Get 'em off!*

(*The light snaps back to normal.*)

CECILY: I don't think you ought to talk to me like that during library hours. However, as the reference section is about to close for lunch I will overlook it. Intellectual curiosity is not so common that one can afford to discourage it. What kind of books were you wanting?

CARR: Books? What books? What do you mean, Cecily, by books? I have read Mr. Lenin's article and I don't need to read any more. I have come to tell you that you seem to me to be the visible personification of absolute perfection.

CECILY: In body or mind?

CARR: In every way.

CECILY: Oh, Tristan!

CARR: You will love me back and tell me all your secrets, won't you?

CECILY: You silly boy! Of course! I have waited for you for
months.

CARR (*amazed*): For months?

CECILY: Ever since Jack told me he had a younger brother who
was a decadent nihilist it has been my girlish dream to
reform you and to love you.

CARR: Oh, Cecily!

(*Her embrace drags him down out of sight behind her desk.
He re-surfaces momentarily——*)

But, my dear Cecily, you don't mean that you couldn't
love me if——

(*—and is dragged down again.*)

(NADYA *enters and comes down to address the audience,
undramatically.*)

NADYA: From the moment news of the revolution came, Ilyich
burned with eagerness to go to Russia . . . He did not sleep,
and at night all sorts of incredible plans were made. We
could travel by aeroplane. But such things could only be
thought of in the semi-delirium of the night. A passport of
a foreigner from a neutral country would have to be
obtained. Letter to Yakov Ganetsky in Stockholm, March
19th, 1917 . . . "I cannot wait any longer. No legal means
of transit available. Whatever happens, Zinoviev and I must
reach Russia. The only possible plan is as follows: you
must find two Swedes who resemble Zinoviev and me, but
since we cannot speak Swedish they must be deaf mutes.
I enclose our photographs for this purpose."

(TZARA *enters.*)

TZARA (*a rising note of incredulity*): Two . . . Swedish . . . deaf
mutes . . . ???

(*He leans his back against the desk.*)

NADYA (*out front, independent of Tzara*): The plan mentioned
in this letter was not realised.

(LENIN *enters, clean shaven and wearing a wig.*)

Letter to V. A. Karpinsky in Geneva, the same day,
March 19th, 1917.

LENIN: My dear Vyacheslav Alexeyevich. I am considering

carefully and from every point of view what will be the best way of travelling to Russia. The following is absolutely secret. I ask you to reply at once, and perhaps it would be best by express (let us hope we will not ruin the party by sending a dozen or more express letters!) so as to be certain no one has read this letter.

(CARR *pops up attentively from behind the desk, and listens carefully*.)

Please procure in your name papers for travelling to France and England. I will use these when passing through England and *Holland* to Russia. I can wear a wig.

The passport photograph will be of *me* in a wig. I shall go to the Berne Consulate to present your papers and I shall be wearing the wig.

(CECILY *appears from behind the desk*.)

You must disappear from Geneva for at least two or three weeks, until you receive a telegram from me in Scandinavia . . . Your Lenin. P.S. . . . I write to you because I am convinced that everything between us will remain *absolutely* secret.

CECILY: Jack!

TZARA (*turning one way*): Cecily!

CECILY: I have such a surprise for you. Your brother is here.

TZARA: What nonsense! I haven't got a brother.

CECILY: Oh, don't say that! He has renounced the life of decadent nihilism which you and Vladimir Ilyich rightly——

TZARA: I don't know what it all means, it is perfectly absurd— (*he turns the other way and sees* CARR)—Oh my God.

(*The* LENINS *stop and stare at these events*.)

CARR: Brother Jack, I have come to tell you that I am sorry for all the embarrassment I have caused you in the past, and that I hope very much that I do not have to embarrass you in the future.

CECILY: Jack, you are not going to refuse your own brother's hand!

TZARA: Nothing will induce me to take his hand. He knows perfectly well why.

(CECILY *runs, weeping, off-stage, followed by* CARR.)

(LENIN *and* NADYA *turn away.* LENIN *takes off his wig in disgust.*)

NADYA: The plan mentioned in this letter was not realised. On the same day, March 19th, there was a meeting of the Russian political emigré groups in Switzerland to discuss ways and means of getting back to Russia.

(CARR *returns as Old Carr. The lighting changes to a* SPOT *on him, dark elsewhere. He takes up* NADYA's *words . . .*)

CARR: On the same day March 19th, there was a meeting of the Russian political emigré groups in Switzerland to discuss ways and means of—sorry about the other business, incidentally, did you notice? Of course you did—hello, hello, you thought, he's doing it again, right well never mind here's the picture: middle of March: Lenin and I in Zurich. I'd got pretty close to him, had a stroke of luck with a certain little lady and I'd got a pretty good idea of his plans, in fact I might have stopped the whole Bolshevik thing in its tracks, but— here's the point. *I was uncertain.* What was the right thing? And then there were my feelings for Cecily. And don't forget, *he wasn't Lenin then! I mean who was he?* as it were. So there I was, the lives of millions of people hanging on which way I'd move, or whether I'd move at all, another man might have cracked—sorry about the other business, incidentally—On the same day, March 19th, there was a meeting of the Russian political emigré groups in Switzerland to discuss ways and means of getting back to Russia . . .

(CARR *exits. Alternatively a projection screen may be lowered in front of him and photos of the various people* NADYA *mentions could be projected.*)

NADYA: Martov suggested obtaining permits for emigrants to pass through Germany in exchange for German and Austrian prisoners of war interned in Russia. But no one wanted to go that way, except Lenin, who snatched at the plan.

LENIN: March 21st, letter to Karpinsky in Geneva: "Martov's plan is good. We ought to begin working for it, only *we* cannot do this directly. We would be suspected . . . But the plan itself is *very* good and *quite* right."

(CARR *re-enters, young again, and comes down and stands next to* TZARA.)

(*The corner of the Stage now occupied by* TZARA *and* CARR *is independent of the* LENINS. *It can no longer be said that the scene is taking place "in the Library".* CARR *and* TZARA *might be in a café; or anywhere.*)

CARR: According to the papers, the man to watch is Kerensky.

NADYA: *Lenin's Journey Through Germany in the Sealed Train*, book by Fritz Platten, Swiss socialist, 1924.

"Since direct contact between the exiles and the German authorities was considered undesirable, it was agreed that Comrade Grimm—President of the Zimmerwald Committee —should undertake the negotiations."

CARR: I should like to make it clear that my feelings for Cecily are genuine.

NADYA: March 25th. Telegram from the German High Command to the Foreign Ministry in Berlin: "No objection to the transit of Russian revolutionaries if effected in special train with reliable escort."

CARR: Look—be fair. The Americans are about to enter the war and it's not a good moment for some Bolshevik to pull the Russians out of it. It could turn the whole thing round. I mean, I *am* on the side of Right. Remember plucky little Poland—not Poland, the other one.

NADYA: March 31st. Telegram to Grimm.

LENIN: "Our party definitely decided to accept plan for Russian emigrants to pass through Germany . . . We absolutely cannot agree to any further delay. Protest strongly against it . . ."

NADYA: Lenin therefore decided to take a hand in the affair himself, through the medium of someone in his confidence. One morning at about eleven a.m., Fritz Platten received a telephone message at the Party Secretariat asking him to go to a discussion with Comrade Lenin at 1.30 p.m. at the Eintract Restaurant. When he got there he found quite a gathering of people round the lunch table. Lenin, Radek, Munzenberg and Platten, then withdrew for a confidential discussion during which Lenin asked Platten——

82

LENIN: Are you prepared to act as our representative in the matter of the journey home and to accompany us on the journey through Germany?

NADYA: After considering the matter for a short time, Platten agreed.

CARR: Anyway, according to Marxist theory, the dialectic of history will get you to much the same place with or without *him*. If Lenin did not exist it would be unnecessary to invent him. Or Marx, for that matter.

LENIN: Telegram to Bolsheviks leaving Scandinavia for St. Petersburg: "Our tactics: no trust in and no support of the new Government. Kerensky is especially suspect. Arming of the proletariat is the only guarantee. Immediate elections to the Petrograd Duma. No rapprochement with other parties. Telegraph this to Petrograd."

NADYA: April 3rd. The German Minister received Platten. He was authorised by Lenin and Zinoviev to present the following conditions to Minister Romberg: (1) That he, Fritz Platten, assume full personal responsibility for escorting the railway carriage. (2) The carriage to be allowed extra-territorial rights. (3) No passport control or check. (4) . . .

CARR: Furthermore I don't understand your interest. All this dancing attendance on Marxism is sheer pretension. You're an amiable bourgeois with a chit from Matron and if the revolution came you wouldn't know what hit you. You're nothing. You're an artist. And multi-coloured micturition is no trick to those boys, they'll have you pissing blood.

TZARA: Artists and intellectuals will be the conscience of the revolution. He is a reactionary in art, and in politics he was brought up in a hard school that killed weaker spirits, but he is moved by a vision of a society of free and equal men. And he will listen. He listens to Gorki—do you know Gorki?

CARR: No.

TZARA: Well, do what you will. To a Dadaist history comes out of a hat too.

LENIN: April 7th. Telegram to Ganetsky in Stockholm:

"Twenty of us are leaving tomorrow."

CARR: I don't think there'll be a place for Dada in a Communist society.

TZARA: That's what we have against this one. There's a place for us in it.

NADYA: On April 9th at 2.30 in the afternoon the travellers moved off from the Zahringer Hof Restaurant in true Russian style, loaded with pillows, blankets and a few personal belongings. Ilyich wore a bowler hat, a heavy overcoat and the thick-soled hobnailed boots that had been made for him by the cobbler Kammerer at number 14 Spiegelgasse. Telegram to his sister in St. Petersburg:

LENIN: "Arriving Monday night, eleven. Tell *Pravda*."

(NADYA *and* LENIN *leave*.)

(*Distant sound of train setting off*.)

TZARA: The train left at 3.10, on time.

(TZARA *leaves*.)

CARR (*decisively*): No, it is perfectly clear in my mind. He must be stopped. The Russians have got a government of patriotic and moderate men. Prince Lvov is moderately conservative, Kerensky is moderately socialist, and Guchkov is a businessman. All in all a promising foundation for a liberal democracy on the Western model, and for a vigorous prosecution of the war on the Eastern front, followed by a rapid expansion of trade. I shall telegraph the Minister in Berne.

(CARR *leaves*.)

(*The train noise becomes very loud*.)

(*Everything black except a light on* LENIN. *He is bearded again. There is a much reproduced photograph of Lenin addressing the crowd in a public square in May 1920—* "balding, bearded, in the three-piece suit" *as Carr describes him; he stands as though leaning into a gale, his chin jutting, his hands gripping the edge of the rostrum which is waist-high, the right hand at the same time gripping a cloth cap . . . a justly famous image. (This is the photo, incidentally, which Stalin had re-touched so as to expunge Kamenev and Trotsky who feature prominently in the original.)*)

(The image on stage now recalls this photograph.)
(The screen, if one is used, now disappears. It is structurally important to the Act that the following speech is delivered from the strongest possible position with the most dramatic change of effect from the general stage appearance preceding it. Ideally LENIN *should speak from a high rostrum, possibly using Cecily's desk, or a bookcase.)*
*(*LENIN, *as the orator, is now the only person on stage.)*

LENIN: Today, literature must become party literature. Down with non-partisan literature! Down with literary supermen! Literature must become a part of the common cause of the proletariat, a cog in the Social Democratic mechanism . . . I dare say there will be hysterical intellectuals to raise a howl at this . . . Such outcries would be nothing more than an expression of bourgeois-intellectual individualism.

Publishing and distributing centres, bookshops and reading rooms, libraries and similar establishments must all be under party control. We want to establish and we shall establish a free press, free not simply from the police, but also from capital, from careerism, and what is more, *free from bourgeois anarchist individualism!* These last words may seem paradoxical or an affront to my audience. Calm yourselves, ladies and gentlemen! Everyone is free to write and say whatever he likes, without any restrictions. *But* every voluntary association, including the party, is also free to expel members who use the name of the party to advocate anti-party views. Secondly, we must say to you bourgeois individualists that your talk about absolute freedom is sheer hypocrisy. There can be no real and effective freedom in a society based on the power of money. Are you free in relation to your bourgeois publisher, Mr. Writer? And in relation to your bourgeois public which demands that you provide it with pornography? The freedom of the bourgeois writer, artist or actor is simply disguised dependence on the money-bag, on corruption, on prostitution. Socialist literature and art will be free because the idea of socialism and sympathy with the working people, instead of greed and careerism, will bring ever new forces to its ranks. It will be free because it will serve not some satiated heroine, not the bored upper ten thousand suffering from fatty degeneration, but the millions and tens of millions of working people, the flower of the country, its strength and its future.

(*A climactic note, and a* LIGHT CUE *which reveals* NADYA *standing downstage and which changes the ambience into something less public, more interior.* LENIN *disappears.*)

NADYA: Ilyich wrote those remarks in 1905 during the first revolution. He wrote very little about art and literature, generally, but he enjoyed it. We sometimes went to concerts and the theatre, even the music hall—he laughed a lot at the clowns—and he was moved to tears when we saw *La Dame aux Camelias* in London in 1907. Gorki tells us in his *Days with Lenin* how Ilyich admired Tolstoy, which is true, of course, especially *War and Peace*, but, as Ilyich put it in an article in 1908 on Tolstoy's 80th birthday . . .

LENIN (*entering*): . . . On the one hand we have the great artist; on the other hand we have the landlord obsessed with Christ. On the one hand the strong and sincere protester against social injustice, and on the other hand the jaded hysterical sniveller known as the Russian intellectual, beating his breast in public and wailing, "I am a bad wicked man, but I am practising moral self-perfection. I don't eat meat, I now eat rice cutlets." On the one hand, merciless criticism of capitalist exploitation, on the other hand the crackpot preaching of submission and of one of the most odious things on earth, namely religion. Tolstoy reflected the stored-up hatred and the readiness for a new future—and at the same time the immature dreaming and political flabbiness which was one of the main causes for the failure of the 1905 revolution.

NADYA: However he respected Tolstoy's traditional values as an artist. The *new* art seemed somehow alien and incomprehensible to him. Clara Zetkin, in her memoirs, remembers him bursting out.

LENIN: Bosh and nonsense! We are good revolutionaries but we seem to be somehow obliged to keep up with modern art.

86

Well, as for me I'm a barbarian. Expressionism, futurism, cubism . . . I don't understand them and I get no pleasure from them.

NADYA: Once, in 1919, we went to a concert in the Kremlin and an actress started declaiming something by Mayakovsky . . . Mayakovsky was celebrated even before the revolution, when he used to shout his fractured lines in a yellow blazer with blue roses painted on his cheeks. Ilyich was in the front row, and he nearly jumped out of his skin.

LENIN: Memo to A. V. Lunacharsky, Commissar for Education—"Aren't you ashamed for printing 5,000 copies of Mayakovsky's new book? It is nonsense, stupidity, double-dyed stupidity and affectation. I believe such things should be published one in ten, and not more than 1,500 copies, for librarians and cranks. As for Lunacharsky, he should be flogged for his futurism."

NADYA: One evening Ilyich wanted to see for himself how the young people were getting on in the communes. I think it was the day Kropotkin was buried in 1921. It was a hungry year but the young people were filled with enthusiasm and their joy was reflected in his face.

LENIN: What do you read?—do you read Pushkin?

NADYA: "Oh no," said someone, "after all, he was a bourgeois. We read Mayakovsky."

LENIN: I think that Pushkin is better.

NADYA: After this, Ilyich took a more favourable view of Mayakovsky. He admitted that he was not a competent judge of poetical talent. Ilyich was much more concerned with the question of bourgeois intellectuals.

LENIN: February 13, 1908, to Gorki, Dear Alexei Maximych . . . I think that some of the questions you raise about our differences of opinion are a sheer misunderstanding. Never of course, have I thought of, quote, persecuting the intelligentsia . . . or of denying that the intelligentsia is necessary to the workers' movement . . .

NADYA: Gorki joined the Democratic Party before 1905, and supported it with his earnings. Ilyich liked Gorki the man and he liked Gorki the artist. He said that Gorki the artist was capable of grasping things instantly. With Gorki he always spoke very frankly.

LENIN: September 15, 1919, to A. M. Gorki, Dear Alexei Maximych . . . Even before receiving your letter we had decided in the Central Committee to appoint Kamenev and Bukharin to check on the arrests of bourgeois intellectuals of the near-Cadet type, and to release whoever possible. For it is clear to us too that there have been mistakes here.

It is also clear that in general the measure of arrest has been necessary and correct. Reading your frank opinion of this matter, I recall a remark of yours which stuck in my mind during our talks (in London, on Capri, and later)— namely: "We artists are irresponsible people." Exactly! You utter incredibly angry words—about what? About a few dozen (or perhaps even a few hundred) Cadet and near-Cadet gentry spending a few days in jail in order to prevent plots which threaten the lives of tens of thousands of workers and peasants. A calamity indeed! What an injustice! A few days, or even weeks, in jail for intellectuals in order to prevent the massacre of tens of thousands of workers and peasants. "Artists are irresponsible people!" Both on Capri and afterwards, I told you—you allow yourself to be surrounded by the very worst elements of bourgeois intelligentsia and succumb to their whining.

No, really, you will go under if you don't tear yourself away from these bourgeois intellectuals. With all my heart I wish that you do this quickly. All the best. Yours, Lenin. P.S. For you are not writing anything! For an artist to waste himself on the whining of rotting intellectuals—is it not ruinous and shameful?

NADYA: I remember when we were in London in 1903 how Ilyich wished he could go to the Moscow Art Theatre to see *The Lower Depths*. We did so after the Revolution. It goes without saying that he set high standards for a Gorki production. Well, the over-acting irritated him. After seeing *The Lower Depths* he avoided the theatre for a long time. But once we went to see *Uncle Vanya*, which he liked very much. And finally the last time we went to the theatre, in 1922, we saw a stage version of Charles Dickens's *Cricket on the Hearth*. After the first act, Ilyich found it dull. The saccharine sentimentality got on his nerves, and during the conversation between the old toymaker and his blind daughter he could stand it no longer and we left.

(*The "Appassionata" Sonata of Beethoven is quietly introduced.*)

But I remember him one evening at a friend's house in Moscow, listening to a Beethoven Sonata . . .

LENIN: I don't know of anything greater than the Appassionata. Amazing, superhuman music. It always makes me feel, perhaps naïvely, it makes me feel proud of the miracles that human beings can perform. But I can't listen to music often. It affects my nerves, makes me want to say nice stupid things and pat the heads of those people who while living in this vile hell can create such beauty. Nowadays we can't pat heads or we'll get our hands bitten off. We've got to *hit* heads, hit them without mercy, though ideally we're against doing violence to people . . . Hm, one's duty is infernally hard . . .

(*The* LIGHT GOES OUT *on him. He leaves.*)

(*The music continues.*)

NADYA: Once when Vladimir was in prison—in St. Petersburg— he wrote to me and asked that at certain times of day I should go and stand on a particular square of pavement on the Shpalernaya. When the prisoners were taken out for exercise it was possible through one of the windows in the corridor to catch a momentary glimpse of this spot. I went for several days and stood a long while on the pavement there. But he never saw me. Something went wrong. I forget what.

(*The "Appassionata" swells in the dark to cover the set-change to "The Room".* GWEN *is seated. There are tea things on the table. The "Appassionata" degenerates absurdly into "Mr. Gallagher and Mr. Shean."* BENNETT *enters, followed by* CECILY.)

(*The rhyme-scheme of the song is fairly evident. The verses are of ten lines each, the first line being a non-rhyming primer. The fourth and fifth verses may be omitted in performance.*)

BENNETT: Miss Carruthers . . .

CECILY: Cecily Carruthers . . .

GWEN: Cecily Carruthers! What a pretty name!
        According to the Consul
        'Round the fashionable fonts you'll
        often hear the Cecily's declaimed.

CECILY: Oh dear Miss Carr, oh dear Miss Carr,
        pleasure remain exactly where you are—
        I beg you don't get up——

GWEN: (*to* BENNETT) I think we'll need another cup—
        Pray sit down, Miss Carruthers,

CECILY: So kind of you, Miss Carr.
        (*Exit* BENNETT.)

GWEN: Miss Carruthers, oh Miss Carruthers . . .
        I hope that you will call me Gwendolen.
        I feel I've known you long
        And I'm never ever wrong—
        Something tells me that we're going to be great
                                          friends.

CECILY: (*upper class*) Oh, Gwendolen! Oh, Gwendolen!
        It sounds ez pretty *ez* a mendolen!
        I hope that you'll feel free
        to call me Cecily . . .

GWEN: Absolutely, Cecily.

CECILY: Then that's settled Gwendolen.

CECILY: Oh, Gwendolen, Oh, Gwendolen . . .
        I fear you don't remember where we met.
        I'm not so picturesque
        when seen behind a desk——

GWEN: Of *course*, my dear—*how* could I forget?
        Oh, Cecily, Oh, Cecily,
        Accept my sincere apology!
        Now be absolutely frank,
        is there trouble at the bank?

90

CECILY: At the Libr'ry, Gwendolen.
GWEN: At the *Libr'ry*, Cecily!

CECILY: Oh Gwendolen, Oh Gwendolen . . .
        I dread to state the reason for my call.
        The fact is there's a fee
        due on Homer's *Odyssey*
        and the *Irish Times* for June 1904.
GWEN: Oh Cecily, Oh Cecily,
        A friend of mine is writing *Ulysses*!
        I'm sure he never knew
        that the books were overdue——
CECILY: Since October, Gwendolen.
GWEN: On my ticket, Cecily!
        (*Enter* BENNETT *with cup. There is a certain amount of tea-
        pouring and tea-sipping to come, not to mention the cup
        suddenly clinked down on the saucer, and all that; but
        directions to this effect are omitted.*)
GWEN: Oh Cecily, Oh Cecily . . .
        Aren't you the girl who has that Russian friend?
        I pass him every day
        by Economics A to K——
CECILY: (*sadly*) It's never going to be the same again.
        Oh Gwendolen, Oh Gwendolen!
        He left this afternoon on the three-ten.
        I've just come from the train.
        But we'll hear of him again . . .
GWEN: (*insincerely*) Absolutely, Cecily . . .
CECILY: *Positively*, Gwendolen!
        (*Exit* BENNETT.)
CECILY: Oh Gwendolen, Oh Gwendolen . . .
        The Library is going to seem so sad.
        Apart from Mr. Tzara
        all the Bolsheviki are a-
        board that special choo-choo bound for Petrograd.
GWEN: Excuse me, Cecily, dear Cecily . . .
        This Mr. Tzara, does he spell it with a T?
        T-Z-A-R-A?

A Bolshevik, you say?

CECILY: Absolutely, Gwendolen.

GWEN: You surprise me, Cecily.

GWEN: Oh Cecily, oh Cecily . . .
I must admit you've taken me aback.
I shall certainly insist on
a tête-à-tête with Tristan——

CECILY: With Tristan?—No, I mean his brother Jack.
Oh Gwendolen, Oh Gwendolen!
Tristan's quite another thing again.

GWEN: Brother Jack is news to me——

CECILY: They kept it in the family——

GWEN: Relatively, Cecily.

CECILY: Imminently, Gwendolen.

CECILY: Oh Gwendolen, Oh Gwendolen
I'd like you to be the first to know . . .
Tristan's hanging up his hat
for the proletariat.
We have an understanding——

GWEN: (*rising*) Just a mo-
(*sitting*) ment, Cecily, dear Cecily,
Tristan's understanding is with me.
What he writes (or draws)
is no concern of yours.

CECILY: Relatively, Gwendolen——

GWEN: *Absolutely*, Cecily!

GWEN: Oh, Cecily . . . Oh Cecily . . .
you have made an unfortunate mistake.
Forgive me if I say
Tristan mentioned yesterday
he delectates his art for its own sake.

CECILY: Oh Gwendolen, Oh Gwendolen
Clearly he has changed his mind since then.
Today he said, "My heart's
no longer in the arts

excepting, Cecily, as a means towards an end."

GWEN: (*frigid*) Oh Cecily, Oh Cecily . . .
To say this gives me physical distress
but one of Joyce's chapters
sent Tristan into raptures
on the subject of the stream of consciousness.

CECILY: Oh Gwendolen, Oh Gwendolen,
it harrows me to contradict a friend,
but his consciousness of class
is the one that's going to last——

GWEN: Lower middle, Cecily?

CECILY: Are you really, Gwendolen?

GWEN: (*rising*) Miss Carruthers,

CECILY: (*ditto*)   Yes, Miss Carr.

GWEN: I do not wish to trespass on your time.

CECILY: I hope that I will see
you at the Library
should you ever get around to pay your fine.
Miss Carr. (*bows.*)
    (*To the door.*)

GWEN: Miss Carruthers,
Is it done to wish you luck with all the others?
I'm not awfully au fait
with manners down your way——

CECILY: And up yours, Miss Carr—*Tristan!*
    (CARR *has entered. Pause.*)

GWEN: (*censoriously*)   That's my
                                           brother.

CECILY: Your brother?

GWEN: Yes. My brother, Henry Carr.

CECILY: Do you mean that he is not Tristan Tzara the artist?

GWEN: Quite the contrary. He is the British Consul.
    (CARR *has frozen like a hunting dog. He is holding the folder
    given to him by* CECILY *in the Library.* BENNETT *opens the
    door.*)

BENNETT: Mr. Tzara . . .

(TRISTAN *enters.* BENNETT *retires.* TZARA *carries his folder.*)

GWEN: Tristan! My Tristan!

CECILY: Comrade Jack!

GWEN: Comrade Jack?

CECILY: Yes. The gentleman who has his arm round your waist is a luminary of the Zimmerwald Left.

GWEN: Are they Bolsheviks?

CECILY: Well, they dine with us.

GWEN: A gross deception has been practised upon us. My poor wounded Cecily!

CECILY: My sweet wronged Gwendolen!
(*They are making for the door.*)

CECILY (*halting*): There is just one question I should like to ask Mr. Carr.

GWEN: An admirable idea. Mr. Tzara, there is a question I should like to put to you.

CECILY: What in truth *was* your opinion of the essay I gave you to read?

GWEN: What indeed *did* you think of the chapter I showed you?

CARR (*timidly*): Very . . . well written . . . Interesting style . . .

TZARA (*timidly*): Very . . . well read . . . Rich material.

CECILY: But as a social critique——?

GWEN: But as art for art's sake——?

CARR (*giving up*): *Rubbish!* He's a madman!

TZARA: Bilge! It's unreadable!

GWEN & CECILY: Oh! Hypocrites!

CARR: I'm sorry! 'Twas for love!

GWEN & CECILY: For love?

GWEN: That is true . . .

CECILY: Yes, it is.
(*In unison they move towards the men, then in unison change their minds.*)

GWEN & CECILY: But our intellectual differences are an insuperable barrier!
(*The door closes behind them.*)
(CARR *and* TZARA *sink into the two main chairs.*)

CARR: By the way, I hear that Bennett has been showing you my private correspondence.

(BENNETT *enters with champagne for two on a tray. He begins to dispense it.*)

TZARA: He has radical sympathies.

CARR: There is no one so radical as a manservant whose freedom of the champagne bin has been interfered with.

TZARA: So I believe.

CARR: Well, I've put a stop to it.

TZARA: Given him notice?

CARR: Given him more champagne.

TZARA: We Rumanians have much to learn from the English.

CARR: I expect you'll be missing Sofia.

TZARA: You mean Gwendolen.

CARR (*frowns; clears*): Bucharest.

TZARA: Oh, yes, Yes. The Paris of the Balkans . . .

CARR: Silly place to put it, really . . . (*sips*) Is this the Perrier-Jouet, Brut, '89?????!!!

BENNETT: No, sir.

CARR (*he has read the writing on the wall*): All gone . . . ?

BENNETT (*implacably*): I'm afraid so, sir.

CARR: Very well, Bennett.

BENNETT: I have put the newspapers and telegrams on the sideboard, sir.

CARR: Anything of interest?

BENNETT: The *Neue Zuricher Zeitung* and the *Zuricher Post* announce respectively the cultural high and low point of the theatrical season at the Theater zur Kaufleuten yesterday evening. The *Zeitung* singles you out for a personal triumph in a demanding role. The Minister telegraphs his congratulations, and also thanks you for your telegram to him. He urges you to prevent Mr. Ulyanov leaving Switzerland at all costs.

(BENNETT *leaves.* PAUSE.)

CARR: Irish lout . . .

TZARA: Russian . . .

CARR: No—whatsisname—Deidre.

TZARA: Bridget . . . (*pause*)

CARR: Joyce!

TZARA: Joyce!

95

CARR: Lout. Quadri-oculate Irish git . . . Came round to the dressing room and handed me ten francs like a *tip*—bloody nerve—Sponger——

(BENNETT *enters.*)

BENNETT: Mr. Joyce.

(JOYCE *enters in an agitated state.*)

JOYCE: Where is your sister?

CARR: Her money is in trust.

JOYCE: I have only one request to make of *you*——

CARR: And I have only one request to make of *you—why for God's sake cannot you contrive just once to wear the jacket that is suggested by your trousers??*

(*It is indeed the case that* JOYCE *is now wearing the other halves of the outfit he wore in Act One.*)

JOYCE (*with dignity*): If I could do it once, I could do it every time. My wardrobe got out of step in Trieste, and its reciprocal members pass each other endlessly in the night. Now—could you let me have the twenty-five francs.

CARR: What twenty-five francs?

JOYCE: You were given eight tickets to sell at five francs per ticket. My books indicate that only fifteen francs has been received from you.

CARR: I have spent three hundred and fifty francs of my own money so that your off-the-peg production should boast one character who looked as if he was acquainted with a tailor. If you hope to get a further twenty-five francs out of me you will have to drag me through the courts. (*deliberately*) *You are a swindler and a cad!*

TZARA (*handing* JOYCE *his folder*): Furthermore, your book has much in common with your dress. As an arrangement of words it is graceless without being random; as a narrative it lacks charm or even vulgarity; as an experience it is like sharing a cell with a fanatic in search of a mania.

(GWEN *and* CECILY *enter.* JOYCE *is scanning the manuscript.*)

JOYCE: Who gave you this manuscript to read?

GWEN: I did!

JOYCE: Miss Carr, did I or did I not give you to type a chapter in which Mr. Bloom's adventures correspond to the

Homeric episode of the Oxen of the Sun?

GWEN: Yes, you did! And it was wonderful!

JOYCE: Then why do you return to me an ill-tempered thesis purporting to prove, amongst other things, that Ramsay MacDonald is a bourgeois lickspittle gentleman's gentleman?

GWEN: (Aaaah)

TZARA: (Ohhhh)

CECILY: (Oops!)

CARR: (Aaah!)

JOYCE (*thunders*): Miss Carr, where is the missing chapter???

CARR: Excuse me—did you say Bloom?

JOYCE: I did.

CARR: And is it a chapter, inordinate in length and erratic in style, remotely connected with midwifery?

JOYCE: It is a chapter which by a miracle of compression, uses the gamut of English literature from Chaucer to Carlyle to describe events taking place in a lying-in hospital in Dublin.

CARR (*holding out his folder*): It is obviously the same work.
(GWEN *and* CECILY *swap folders with cries of recognition.* CARR *and* TZARA *close in. A rapid but formal climax, with appropriate cries of "Cecily! Gwendolen! Henry! Tristan!" and appropriate embraces.*)
(*Music, appropriate to the period. Light change. A formal, short dance sequence.* TZARA *dances with* GWEN, CARR *with* CECILY. JOYCE *and* BENNETT *dance independently. The effect is of course a complete dislocation of the play.* CARR *and* CECILY *dance out of view. The others continue, and then they, too, dance offstage just as* OLD CARR *dances back on stage with* OLD CECILY.
(OLD CECILY *is about 80 of course, like Old Carr. They dance a few decrepit steps.*)

OLD CECILY: No, no, no, no it's pathetic though there was a court case I admit, and your trousers came into it, I don't deny, but you never got close to Vladimir Ilyich, and I don't remember the other one. I do remember Joyce, yes you are quite right and he was Irish with glasses but that was the year after—1918—and the train had long gone from

the station! I waved a red hanky and cried long live the
revolution as the carriage took him away in his bowler hat
and yes, I said yes when you asked me, but he was the
leader of millions by the time you did your Algernon . . .

CARR: Algernon—that was him.

OLD CECILY: I said that was the year after——

CARR: After what?

OLD CECILY: You never even saw Lenin.

CARR: Yes I did. Saw him in the cafés. I knew them all. Part
of the job.

OLD CECILY (*small pause*): And you were never the Consul.

CARR: Never said I was.

OLD CECILY: Yes you did.

CARR: Should we have a cup of tea?

OLD CECILY: The Consul was Percy somebody.

CARR: (Bennett.)

OLD CECILY: What?

CARR (*testily*): I said the Consul's name was Bennett!

OLD CECILY: Oh yes . . . Bennett . . . (*pause*) That's another
thing——

CARR: *Are we going to have a cup of tea or not?*

OLD CECILY: And I never helped him write *Imperialism, the
Highest Stage of Capitalism*. That was the year before, too.
1916.

CARR: Oh, Cecily. I wish I'd known then that you'd turn out to
be a pedant! (*getting angry*) Wasn't this—Didn't do that—
1916—1917—*What of it?* I was here. They were here. They
went on. I went on. We all went on.

OLD CECILY: No, we didn't. We stayed. Sophia married that
artist. I married you. You played Algernon. They all went
on.

(*Most of the fading light is on* CARR *now.*)

CARR: Great days . . . Zurich during the war. Refugees, spies,
exiles, painters, poets, writers, radicals of all kinds. I knew
them all. Used to argue far into the night . . . at the Odeon,
the Terrasse . . . I learned three things in Zurich during
the war. I wrote them down. Firstly, you're either a
revolutionary or you're not, and if you're not you might as

well be an artist as anything else. Secondly, if you can't be an artist, you might as well be a revolutionary . . .

I forget the third thing.

(BLACKOUT.)

Selected List of Grove Press Drama and Theater Paperbacks

E471   BECKETT, SAMUEL / Cascando and Other Short Dramatic Pieces (Words and Music, Film, Play, Come and Go, Eh Joe, Endgame) / $1.95

E96   BECKETT, SAMUEL / Endgame / $1.95

E318   BECKETT, SAMUEL / Happy Days / $2.45

E226   BECKETT, SAMUEL / Krapp's Last Tape, plus All That Fall, Embers, Act Without Words I and II / $2.45

E33   BECKETT, SAMUEL / Waiting For Godot / $1.95 [See also Seven Plays of the Modern Theater, Harold Clurman, ed. GT422 / $4.95]

B117   BRECHT, BERTOLT / The Good Woman of Setzuan / $1.95

B108   BRECHT, BERTOLT / Mother Courage and Her Children / $1.50

B333   BRECHT, BERTOLT / The Threepenny Opera / $1.45

E130   GENET, JEAN / The Balcony / $2.95 [See also Seven Plays of the Modern Theater, Harold Clurman, ed. GT422 / $4.95]

E208   GENET, JEAN / The Blacks: A Clown Show / $2.95

E577   GENET, JEAN / The Maids and Deathwatch: Two Plays / $2.95

E374   GENET, JEAN / The Screens / $1.95

E101   IONESCO, EUGENE / Four Plays (The Bald Soprano, The Lesson, The Chairs,* Jack, or The Submission) / $1.95 *[See also Eleven Short Plays of the Modern Theater, Samuel Moon, ed. B107 / $2.45]

E259   IONESCO, EUGENE / Rhinoceros* and Other Plays (The Leader, The Future is in Eggs, or It Takes All Sorts to Make a World) / $1.95 *[See also Seven Plays of the Modern Theater, Harold Clurman, ed. GT422 / $4.95]

E119   IONESCO, EUGENE / Three Plays (Amédée, The New Tenant, Victims of Duty) / $2.95

B354   PINTER, HAROLD / Old Times / $1.95

E299   PINTER, HAROLD / The Caretaker* and The Dumb Waiter: Two Plays / $1.95 *[See also Modern British Drama, Henry Popkin, ed. GT422 / $5.95]

E411   PINTER, HAROLD / The Homecoming / $1.95

E626   STOPPARD, TOM / Jumpers / $1.95

B319   STOPPARD, TOM / Rosencrantz and Guildenstern Are Dead / $1.95

GROVE PRESS, INC., 196 West Houston Street, New York, N.Y. 10014